Microsoft

T0073753

Microsoft
Teams
Step by Step

Paul McFedries

Microsoft Teams Step By Step
Published with the authorization of Microsoft Corporation by: Pearson Education, Inc.
Copyright © 2023 by Pearson Education, Inc.

ISBN-13: 978-0-13-752218-7
ISBN-10: 0-13-752218-5

Library of Congress Control Number: 2022939632

1 2022

Trademarks

Warning and Disclaimer

Special Sales
For information about buying this title in bulk quantities, or for special sales opportunities (which may include electronic versions; custom cover designs; and content particular to your business, training goals, marketing focus, or branding interests), please contact our corporate sales department at corpsales@pearsoned.com or (800) 382-3419.

For government sales inquiries, please contact governmentsales@pearsoned.com. For questions about sales outside the U.S., please contact intlcs@pearson.com.

Editor-in-Chief
Brett Bartow

Executive Editor
Loretta Yates

Sponsoring Editor
Charvi Arora

Development Editor
Rick Kughen

Managing Editor
Sandra Schroeder

Senior Project Editor
Tracey Croom

Copy Editor
Rick Kughen

Indexer
Valerie Haynes Perry

Proofreader
Dan Foster

Technical Editor
Joan Lambert

Editorial Assistant
Cindy Teeters

Compositor
Danielle Foster

Cover Designer
Twist Creative, Seattle

Image Credits
Figure 8.13(a): HONGQI ZHANG/123RF
Figure 8.13(b): Brett Rabideau/Shutterstock
Figure 8.13(c): goodluz/Shutterstock
Figure 8.13(d): SnowWhiteimages/Shutterstock
Figure 8.13(e): DmitryStock/Shutterstock

Pearson's Commitment to Diversity, Equity, and Inclusion

Pearson is dedicated to creating bias-free content that reflects the diversity of all learners. We embrace the many dimensions of diversity, including but not limited to race, ethnicity, gender, socioeconomic status, ability, age, sexual orientation, and religious or political beliefs.

Education is a powerful force for equity and change in our world. It has the potential to deliver opportunities that improve lives and enable economic mobility. As we work with authors to create content for every product and service, we acknowledge our responsibility to demonstrate inclusivity and incorporate diverse scholarship so that everyone can achieve their potential through learning. As the world's leading learning company, we have a duty to help drive change and live up to our purpose to help more people create a better life for themselves and to create a better world.

Our ambition is to purposefully contribute to a world where:

- Everyone has an equitable and lifelong opportunity to succeed through learning.

- Our educational products and services are inclusive and represent the rich diversity of learners.

- Our educational content accurately reflects the histories and experiences of the learners we serve.

- Our educational content prompts deeper discussions with learners and motivates them to expand their own learning (and worldview).

While we work hard to present unbiased content, we want to hear from you about any concerns or needs with this Pearson product so that we can investigate and address them.

Please contact us with concerns about any potential bias at https://www.pearson.com/report-bias.html.

Contents at a glance

Contents

Acknowledgments

Substitute damn *every time you're inclined to write* very; *your editor will delete it and the writing will be just as it should be.*

—Mark Twain

I didn't follow Mark Twain's advice in this book (the word *very* appears throughout), but if my writing still appears "just as it should be," then it's because of the keen minds and sharp linguistic eyes of the editors at Microsoft Press. Near the front of the book you'll find a long list of the hard-working professionals whose fingers made it into this particular paper pie. However, there are a few folks I worked with directly, so I'd like to single them out for extra credit. A big, heaping helping of thanks goes out to executive editor Loretta Yates, sponsoring editor Charvi Arora, development and copy editor Rick Kughen, production editor Tracey Croom, and technical editor Joan Lambert.

About the author

Paul McFedries is a full-time technical writer. Paul has been authoring computer books since 1991 and has more than 100 books to his credit, which combined have sold more than 4 million copies worldwide. His titles include the Microsoft Press books *MOS Study Guide for Microsoft Excel Expert Exam MO-201*, *MOS Study Guide for Microsoft Access Expert Exam MO-500*, and *MOS Study Guide for Microsoft Word Expert Exam MO-101*. Please drop by Paul's personal website at paulmcfedries.com or follow Paul on Twitter (twitter.com/paulmcf) and Facebook (facebook.com/PaulMcFedries).

Introduction

Available with a standalone subscription or as part of the Microsoft 365 suite of programs, Microsoft Teams is a full-featured communication and collaboration app that enables you to quickly build teams of people and exchange messages, share files, work with apps, place calls, and conduct online video meetings. (There's also a free version of Teams, which is available for online download and is installed with every Windows 11 PC, that offers a subset of the features of the full Teams app.) *Microsoft Teams Step by Step* offers a comprehensive look at the features of Teams that most people will use most frequently.

Who this book is for

Microsoft Teams Step by Step and other books in the *Step by Step* series are designed for beginning- to intermediate-level computer users. Examples shown in the book generally pertain to small and medium businesses but teach skills that can be used in organizations of any size. Whether you are new to Teams or are already comfortable working in Teams and want to learn about new features, this book provides invaluable step-by-step guidance so that you can get the most out of the teams you work with and even create and manage your own teams.

The *Step by Step* approach

The book's coverage is divided into chapters representing skill set areas of Microsoft Teams, such as teams (Chapter 2), channels (Chapters 3 and 4), chat (Chapter 7), and meetings (Chapters 8 through 10). Each chapter is divided into topics that group related skills, and each topic includes expository information followed by generic procedures. At the end of each chapter, you'll find a review of the skills taught in the chapter.

Features and conventions

This book has been designed to lead you step by step through tasks you're likely to want to perform in Teams. The topics are all self-contained, so you can start at the beginning and work your way through all the procedures or reference them independently. If you later need help remembering how to perform a procedure, the following features of this book will help you locate specific information:

- **Detailed table of contents**   Browse the listing of the topics, sections, and sidebars within each chapter.

- **Chapter thumb tabs and running heads**   Identify the pages of each chapter by the thumb tabs on the book's open fore-edge. Find a specific chapter by number or title by looking at the running heads at the top of even-numbered (verso) pages.

- **Topic-specific running heads**   Within a chapter, quickly locate the topic you want by looking at the running heads at the top of odd-numbered (recto) pages.

- **Detailed index**   Look up coverage of specific tasks and features in the index at the back of the book.

You can save time when reading this book by understanding how the *Step by Step* series provides procedural instructions and auxiliary information and identifies on-screen and physical elements that you interact with. The following table lists content formatting conventions used in this book.

Convention	Meaning
TIP	Provides a helpful hint or shortcut to simplify a task.
IMPORTANT	Alerts you to a common problem or provides information necessary to successfully complete a procedure.
SEE ALSO	Directs you to more information about a topic in this book or elsewhere.
1. Numbered steps 2.	Guide you through generic multi-step procedures.
■ Bulleted lists	Indicate single-step procedures and sets of multiple alternative procedures.

Convention	Meaning
Interface objects	In procedures, semibold black text indicates on-screen elements that you should select (click or tap).
User input	Light semibold formatting identifies specific information that you should enter when completing procedures.
Keyboard shortcuts	A plus sign between two keys indicates that you must select those keys at the same time. For example, "press **Ctrl+P**" directs you to hold down the Ctrl key while you press the P key.
Emphasis and *URLs*	In expository text, italic formatting identifies web addresses and emphasized words or phrases.

E-book edition

If you're reading the e-book edition of this book, you can do the following:

- Search the full text

- Print

- Copy and paste

You can purchase and download the e-book edition from the Microsoft Press Store at *MicrosoftPressStore.com/TeamsStepByStep/detail*.

How this book is organized

This book is divided into thirteen chapters. Chapter 1 contains introductory information that will primarily be of interest to readers who are new to Teams. Chapter 2 shows you how to create and manage your own team. If you do not want to manage your own team, you can skip to Chapter 3 and work through the book from there.

This book has been designed to lead you, step by step, through all the tasks you're most likely to want to perform with Teams. If you start at the beginning and work your way through all the tasks, you will gain enough proficiency to be able to create and work with all the major Teams features. However, each topic is self-contained, so you can jump in anywhere to acquire exactly the skills you need.

Get support and give feedback

We've made every effort to ensure the accuracy of this book and its companion content. We welcome your feedback.

Errata and support

If you discover an error, please submit it to us at *MicrosoftPressStore.com/ MSTeamsSBS365/errata*.

We'll investigate all reported issues, update downloadable content if appropriate, and incorporate necessary changes into future editions of this book.

For additional book support and information, please visit *MicrosoftPressStore.com/ Support*.

For assistance with Microsoft software and hardware, visit the Microsoft Support site at *support.microsoft.com*.

Stay in touch

Let's keep the conversation going! We're on Twitter at *twitter.com/MicrosoftPress*.

Get started with Teams

Communicating with other people is often a complex and inefficient process because there are usually many different channels of communication being used by the participants. Short messages might be exchanged via text messaging; longer messages might occur through email; communications requiring the nuance of voice might necessitate a phone call or video call; collaborating on a document might require uploading that file to a cloud folder and sharing that location with others.

All these technologies work well by themselves but using some or all of them to collaborate on a project or keep members of the same department or family in the loop can get complicated. It would be easier and more efficient if you could bring all these disparate methods of communication and collaboration under a single umbrella.

Microsoft Teams is a communication and collaboration tool that organizes people into groups called *teams*. The members of a team almost always have something in common. For example, they might all be working on the same project, or they might all be part of the same department, division, or company. Although Teams is primarily a business tool, many home users take advantage of Teams' communications tools, where a team might consist of members of the same family, a group of friends, or members of the same sports club or community organization.

In this chapter

- What you can do with Microsoft Teams
- Navigate the Teams web, desktop, and mobile apps
- Change your Teams profile picture
- Make sure your devices work with Teams
- Join an existing team
- View your activity feed
- Set your status
- Leave a team

This chapter introduces you to Microsoft Teams and takes you on tours of the web, desktop, and mobile Teams apps. You also learn how to change your Teams profile picture, make sure your audio and video devices can work with Teams, join an existing team, monitor your Teams activity feed, set your status ,and leave a team.

What you can do with Microsoft Teams

If you use Teams at work, there are a half dozen main activities that you can perform with a business Teams account:

- **Chatting**   You can send messages to other team members via the chat feature, which is available separately and within meetings. You can format chat messages, include emojis, and save and delete chat messages.

- **Collaborating with channels**   A *channel* is a separate area within a team. You use a channel to organize conversations, files, and apps around a particular topic or subject. All teams come with a General channel, but you can add as many channels as your team needs.

- **Meeting**   A *meeting* is a virtual gathering that enables attendees to see and hear each other. Teams enables team members to create an ad hoc meeting from a chat or channel or to schedule a meeting. Once in a meeting, attendees can chat, share content, send reactions, and split into breakout rooms.

- **Calling**   You can make voice calls to other team members, people outside of your team, and Skype users. Depending on your Teams subscription, you might also have a voicemail box. Teams voice calls go over the internet instead of a phone line or cellular service.

- **Sharing files**   Team members can share files and have conversations related to specific files.

- **Working with apps**   You can extend Teams by installing one or more apps that add extra features and capabilities to the Teams app.

It's important to understand that not all Teams subscriptions support all these activities. For example, if you have a free Teams account for personal use, you can't create teams or work with channels, you can't make voice calls or work with apps, and your meetings are restricted to 100 participants and a 60-minute maximum.

1

There are three ways to use Teams: via the web, on your desktop PC or Mac, or on your smartphone or tablet. You interact with Teams by using the web app, desktop app, or mobile app. The next three sections take you on tours of each of the three Teams apps.

> ⚠ **IMPORTANT** You need some sort of Teams account to use any Teams app. If you don't have a Microsoft 365 subscription (which includes free access to the Teams app), there's a free version of Teams you can try. See *https://microsoft.com/microsoft-teams/group-chat-software.*

Navigate the Teams web app

Assuming you've already signed up for either a Microsoft Teams standalone account or a Microsoft 365 account, which includes access to the Teams app, you can use your account credentials to sign in to Teams on the web.

Identify the Teams web app interface elements

The Teams web app offers quite a few interface elements. To help you make sense of the interface, know first that the web app page is divided into three main vertical sections:

- **App bar** This vertical strip along the left edge of the Teams web app page displays an icon for each main Teams feature, such as Activity, Chat, and Teams.

- **Panel** This vertical strip to the right of the app bar displays the items associated with the selected app bar icon. If you select Teams, for example, the Teams panel displays a list of the teams of which you're a member and each team's channels.

- **Content pane** This area displays the content of whatever item you select in the panel. For example, if you select a team channel, you see that channel's tabs, conversations, and other content.

Interface elements of the Microsoft Teams web app

The Teams web app offers quite a few other interface elements. To get the most out of Teams, you must be familiar with the following elements:

- **Microsoft 365 Apps**   Select this button to display a list of apps such as Outlook, Word, Excel, and PowerPoint available with your Microsoft 365 subscription.

- **Settings and more**   Select this button to display a menu of commands that enable you to, among other things, access the web app settings and download the desktop and mobile Teams apps.

1

- **Teams account profile button**   Select this button to access commands related to your Teams account.

- **More added apps**   Select this button to see a list of other apps that are part of your Teams subscription.

- **Download desktop app**   Select this button to download the desktop version of the Teams app.

When you first sign in to the Teams web app, you might see a dialog asking you to turn on desktop notifications. This is a good idea for most people because it helps you stay up to date with what's going on with your team. If you see the dialog asking you to turn on desktop notifications, select **Turn on**, and then when your browser asks you to confirm, select **Allow**.

> **SEE ALSO** Teams gives you quite a few options for customizing your notifications. For more information, see "Customize Teams notifications" in Chapter 12, "Customize Teams."

To sign in to the Teams web app

1. Use your web browser to navigate to *https://teams.microsoft.com*.

2. Enter the email address you used when you signed up for your Teams account, and then click **Next**.

3. Enter your account password, and then click **Sign in**.

4. If you see a dialog asking if you want to stay signed in, click **Yes** if you're using your own computer; click **No**, instead, if you're using a public computer.

> ✅ **TIP** If you're surfing with Microsoft Edge, you can sign in to the browser with your Microsoft account credentials by clicking the avatar that appears near the upper-right corner of the Edge window. After you sign in, Edge will automatically sign you in to Teams (and other Microsoft online apps) in the future.

To sign out of the Teams web app

1. In the upper-right corner of the Teams web app page, select your Teams account profile button (not your Microsoft or Google account profile button in the upper-right corner of the browser).

2. Select **Sign out**.

Navigate the Teams desktop app

Although you can perform almost all Teams tasks using the web app, most people find Teams easier to use and more efficient on the desktop. Depending on your Microsoft 365 subscription and your version of Windows, you might already have the Teams desktop app installed. (If you're on a Mac, you need to download and install the desktop app manually.) To check, select Start, and then examine the Start menu and the All Apps list to see if you see a tile or icon for Microsoft Teams. (Alternatively, use the taskbar's Search feature to search for Teams.) If not, you need to download and then install the desktop version of Teams.

Identify the Teams desktop app interface elements

Launching the Teams desktop app displays a window with several interface elements. To help you make sense of the interface, know first that the desktop app window is divided into three main vertical sections:

- **App bar**   This vertical strip along the left edge of the Teams desktop app displays an icon for each main Teams feature, such as Activity, Chat, and Teams.

- **Panel**   This vertical strip to the right of the app bar displays the items associated with the selected app bar icon. If you select Teams, for example, the Teams panel displays a list of the teams of which you're a member as well as the channels associated with those teams.

- **Content pane**   This area displays the content of whatever item you select in the panel. If you select a team channel, for example, you see the tabs, conversations, and other content of that channel.

Teams account profile button

App bar   Panel   Content pane   Settings and more

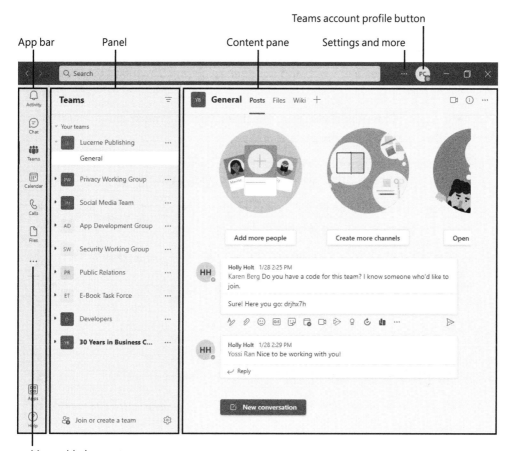

More added apps

Interface elements of the Microsoft Teams desktop app

To get the most out of Teams, you also must be familiar with the following elements of the desktop app:

- **Settings and more**   Select this button to display a menu of commands that enable you to, among other things, access the web app settings and download the desktop and mobile Teams apps.

- **Teams account profile button**   Select this icon to access commands related to your Teams account.

- **More added apps**   Select this icon to see a list of other apps that are part of your Teams subscription.

To download and install the Teams desktop app

1. Download the desktop app using one of the following methods:

   - Sign in to the Teams web app and then select the **Download desktop app** icon.

   - Sign in to the Teams web app, select **Settings and more**, and then select **Download the desktop app**.

   - Use a web browser to navigate to *https://www.microsoft.com/microsoft-teams/download-app* and then select **Download for desktop**.

2. Locate the downloaded file in your computer's **Downloads** folder and double-click the file to launch the setup program.

3. When prompted, sign in to the work or school account you want to use with Teams.

To sign in to the Teams desktop app

1. Select **Start**, select **All apps**, and then select **Microsoft Teams**.

2. Select the Teams account you want to use to sign in.

To sign out of the Teams desktop app

1. Select your Teams account profile button in the top-right corner of the Teams desktop app.

2. Select **Sign out**. Teams signs you out of your account and prompts you to sign in again.

3. Select **Close (X)**.

Navigate the Teams mobile app

If you're out of the office, you don't have to be out of the loop. With the Teams mobile app on your smartphone or tablet, you can continue to communicate and collaborate wherever you are using the Teams mobile app.

You can install the Teams mobile app from the Google Play Store or Apple Store on your mobile device.

Identify the Teams mobile app interface elements

Launching the Teams mobile app displays a window with several interface elements. To get the most out of Teams, you must be familiar with the following elements:

- **Teams account profile button** Select this icon to display a menu of commands that enable you to, among other things, access your account, work with app settings, and set your status.

- **App bar** This horizontal strip along the bottom of the Teams mobile app window displays an icon for each main Teams app, such as Chat, Calls, and Files.

- **More added apps** Select this icon to see a list of other apps that are part of your Teams subscription.

Teams account profile button

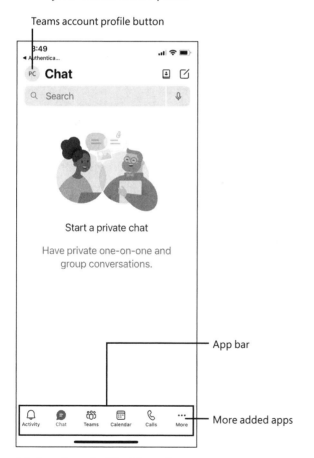

Interface elements of the Microsoft Teams mobile app on a smartphone

To download and install the Teams mobile app

- Do one of the following, depending on your mobile device:

  - On an iOS or iPadOS device, open the App Store and install the Microsoft Teams app.

  - On an Android device, open the Play Store and install the Microsoft Teams app.

To sign in to the Teams mobile app

1. On your device's Home screen, tap **Teams**.

2. Enter the email address you used when you signed up for your Teams account, and then tap **Sign in**.

3. Enter your account password, and then tap **Sign in**.

4. If you see a screen asking you to help Microsoft protect your account, install the Microsoft Authenticator app on your phone and then follow the onscreen prompts to set up and verify your account.

5. If you see a dialog asking for your permission to have Teams send you notifications, tap **Allow**.

6. If you see a dialog asking for your permission to have Teams access your microphone, tap **OK**.

To sign out of the Teams mobile app

1. In the upper-left corner of the Teams mobile app, tap your Teams account profile button.

2. Tap **Settings**.

3. Scroll down if necessary and then tap **Sign out**. Teams asks you to confirm.

4. Tap **OK** or **Sign out**.

Change your Teams profile picture

By default, your Teams profile picture is a circle with your initials inside. One of the first tasks most Teams users perform is to replace that default profile image with a proper photo. You can choose an existing photo from your device, or you can take a new photo using your mobile device camera.

> ⚠ **IMPORTANT** When you change your Teams profile picture, you change the picture for all your Microsoft 365 apps.

To change your profile picture using the Teams web or desktop app

1. In the Teams web or desktop app, select the Teams account profile button.
2. On the **Accounts** page of the **Settings** dialog, select your current profile picture.
3. Select **Upload picture**.
4. In the **Open** dialog, select the image file you want to use for the picture and then select **Open**.

To select an existing photo for your profile picture using the Teams mobile app

1. In the Teams mobile app, tap the Teams account profile button.
2. Tap your name.
3. Tap **Edit image** (Android) or tap your current profile picture (iOS or iPadOS).
4. Tap **Open photo library** (Android) or **Choose existing photo** (iOS or iPadOS). Your device photos appear.
5. Tap the photo you want to use.
6. In iOS or iPadOS, pan and scale the photo as needed.
7. In iOS or iPadOS, tap **Choose**.

To take a new photo for your profile picture using the Teams mobile app

1. In the Teams mobile app, tap the Teams account profile button.
2. Tap your name.
3. Tap **Edit image** (Android) or tap your current profile picture (iOS or iPadOS).
4. Tap **Camera** (Android) or **Take photo** (iOS or iPadOS).
5. If your device asks for permission for Teams to use the camera, tap **OK**.
6. Take the photo and then tap **OK** (Android) or **Use Photo** (iOS or iPadOS). Alternatively, you can tap **Retry** (Android) or **Retake** (iOS or iPadOS) and try again.

Make sure your devices work with Teams

Making calls with Teams requires access to your device speakers and microphone; attending a Teams meeting requires access to both your device's audio hardware and camera. The Teams mobile app uses the default audio and video hardware on the device. However, for the Teams desktop app, you might have multiple speakers, microphones, or cameras, so you need to configure Teams to use the devices you want.

 IMPORTANT If Teams requests access to your mobile device microphone or camera, be sure to allow the access to get the most out of the Teams mobile app.

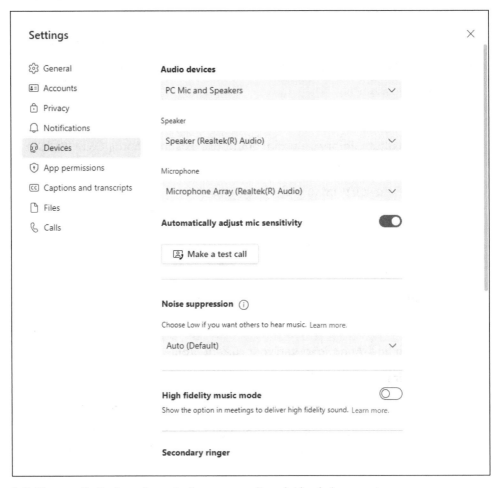

In Settings, use the Devices category to choose your audio and video devices.

To choose your audio devices using the Teams desktop app

1. In the Teams desktop app, select **Settings and more** (...) and then select **Settings**. You can also open Settings by pressing **Ctrl+,** (comma; Windows) or **Cmd+,** (comma; Mac).

2. Select the **Devices** category.

3. Use the **Speaker** list to select the device you want to use for Teams audio output.

4. Use the **Microphone** list to select the device you want to use for Teams audio input.

5. To test your audio devices, select **Make a test call**.

To choose your video device using the Teams desktop app

1. In the Teams desktop app, select **Settings and more** (...) and then select **Settings**. You can also open Settings by pressing **Ctrl+,** (comma; Windows) or **Cmd+,** (comma; Mac).

2. Select the **Devices** category.

3. Use the **Camera** list to select the device you want to use for Teams video.

4. Make sure the live camera feed appears in the **Preview** window.

Join an existing team

When you first sign in to the Teams app, you might see an existing team in the Teams section of the app. (Remember: If you're using a free or home version of Teams, you won't see the Teams section.) This is an organization-wide team created by your Teams administrator, and it includes everyone in your organization. If your organization is small, this might be the only team you need. However, it's more likely that you and your colleagues will require several teams for different projects, departments, events, and groups. You learn how to create your own teams in Chapter 2, "Set up a team."

When a new team is created, the team owner usually adds specific people to the team, and those users are automatically joined once the team is set up. However, if the team owner opted to skip that step, or if the team owner missed some people, the owner can generate a code that enables anyone who has the code to join the team. The team owner might then post the code in a chat, a channel conversation, or an email. If you're not already a team member, you could copy the code and then use it to join the team.

 SEE ALSO To learn how to generate a code that enables people to join a team, see "Generate a team code or link" in Chapter 2, "Set up a team."

Alternatively, the team owner can generate a link to join the team and then share that link via email, text, or social media.

 SEE ALSO To learn how to generate a link that enables people to join a team, see "Generate a team code or link" in Chapter 2, "Set up a team."

TIP If you're a member of many teams, scrolling through the Teams tab to find the team you want can be time-consuming. A faster method in the desktop app is to select the **Search** box, type /goto, type the first few letters of the team name, and then select the team when it appears in the search results.

To join a team with a code using the Teams web or desktop app

1. Copy the team code.

2. In the Teams web or desktop app, select **Teams** in the app bar. In the desktop app, you can also select Teams in the app bar by pressing **Ctrl+3** (Windows) or **Cmd+3** (Mac).

3. Select **Join or create a team** at the bottom of the Teams panel.

4. In the **Enter code** text box, paste the team code.

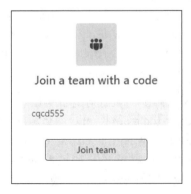

Paste the team code into the text box.

1

5. Select **Join team**. Teams adds you to the team and then displays the team's General channel.

> **TIP** As an alternative to Steps 2 through 5 in the desktop app, select the **Search** box, type /join, type a space, paste the team code, and then select **Join a team with a code** *code*, where *code* is the team code you pasted.

To join a team with a code using the Teams mobile app

1. Copy the team code.

2. In the Teams mobile app, tap **Teams** in the app bar.

3. Tap **+**.

4. Tap **Join a team with a code**.

5. In the **Enter code** text box, paste the team code.

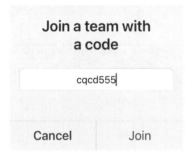

Paste the team code into the text box.

6. Tap **Join**. Teams lets you know you've been added to the team.

7. Tap **OK**.

To join a team with a link using the Teams desktop app

1. Click the link.

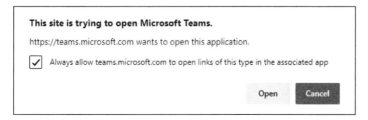

You might see a message similar to this when you click the link to join a team.

2. If you see a message telling you the Teams website is trying to open Microsoft Teams (the message you see depends on the web browser you're using), select the **Always allow teams.microsoft.com to open links of this type in the associated app** checkbox and then select **Open**.

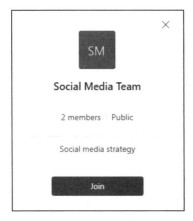

You see this dialog when you open the join link in the Teams desktop app.

3. Select **Join**. Teams adds you to the team.

To join a team with a link using the Teams mobile app

1. Tap the link.

2. Tap **Join team**. Teams adds you to the team.

To join a public team using the Teams web or desktop app

1. In the app bar, select **Teams** in the app bar.

2. Select **Join or create a team** at the bottom of the Teams panel. If you don't see this button, your version of Teams doesn't support this feature.

Select a public team's Join team button to be added to the team.

16

3. On the **Join or create a team** screen, select the public team's **Join team** button. (Note that you don't see the **Join team** button until you hover the mouse pointer over the team's box.) Teams adds you to the team.

 TIP If you don't see the public team you want to join, type some or all of the team's name in the **Search teams** text box and then press **Enter**.

To join a public team using the Teams mobile app

1. In the app bar, tap **Teams**.

2. Tap **Join or create a team**. (In Android, tap the three vertical dots icon in the upper-right corner of the app; in iOS, tap the + icon near the upper-right corner of the app; in iPadOS, tap the + icon near the upper-right corner of the Teams pane.)

3. Tap **Browse team**. Teams displays a list of the available public teams.

4. Tap the **Join** button to the right of the team you want to join. Teams adds you to the team.

View your activity feed

As you work in Teams, the app keeps you up to date with what's happening by keeping track of activities such as the following:

- You're added to a team

- Someone mentions you in a conversation

- Someone replies or reacts to one of your messages

- You miss a call

- You get a voice message

Teams alerts you using two types of notifications:

- **Banner**   This is a pop-up message that appears temporarily in the Teams app.

- **Feed**   These are messages that appear in the **Activity** section of the Teams app. They also generate indicators in the app, such as badges and icons that appear in the app bar and elsewhere.

> **SEE ALSO** Teams gives you quite a few options for customizing your notifications. For more information, see "Customize Teams notifications" in Chapter 12, "Customize Teams."

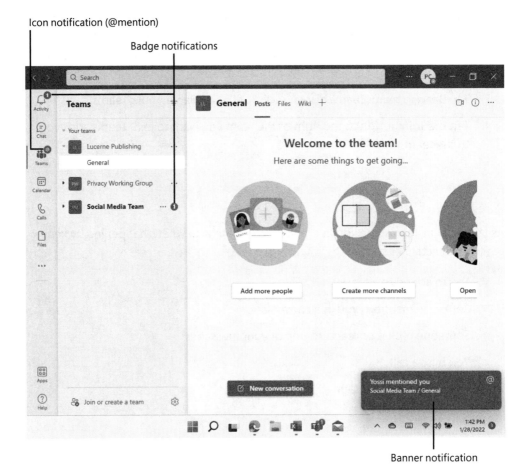

Notifications in the Teams desktop app

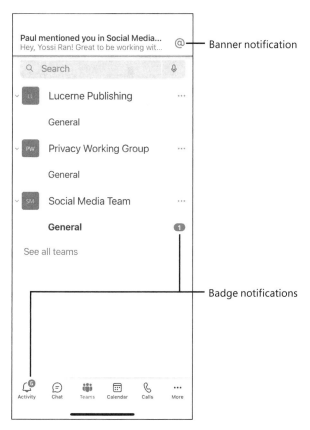

Notifications in the Teams mobile app

To view your activity feed

■ In the Teams web, desktop, or mobile app, select the **Activity** app in the app bar.

■ In the Teams desktop app, press **Ctrl+1** (Windows) or **Cmd+1** (Mac).

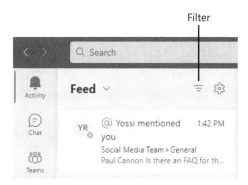

The Activity feed keeps you up to date.

Set your status

Your *status* lets your team members know your availability within Teams. Usually, your status is set to **Available**, which tells team members that if they contact you via chat or channel conversation, you're likely to respond. Conversely, when you're in a meeting, Teams sets your status to **Busy**, so team members can assume that any message sent to you might not be answered right away.

Rather than always letting Teams set your status, you can set it manually to any of the following:

- **Available**   You're available to be contacted. This is the default status when you're not currently in a meeting, call, or other scheduled event.

- **Busy**   You're working in Teams, but you're not currently available. Teams sets this status automatically when you're in a meeting or on a call.

- **Do not disturb**   Disables all notifications. Teams sets this status automatically when you're presenting information in a Teams meeting.

- **Be right back**   Tells team members that you're temporarily unavailable.

- **Appear away**   Tells team members that you're away from your computer or mobile device. Teams sets this status automatically when you lock your device or put it into sleep mode.

- **Appear offline**   Tells Team members that you're not currently signed in to Teams. You still receive notifications, however.

If you want, you can also augment your status with a message. For example, if you set your status to **Be right back**, you might want to also set a status message that says when you'll be available again.

To set your status and an optional status message

1. Select your Teams account profile button.

2. Select your current status. Teams displays the status list.

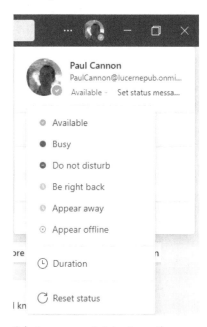

Select your current status to see the status list.

3. Select the status you want to set.

To set an optional status message

1. Select your Teams account profile button.

2. Select **Set status message**.

3. Type your status message.

4. In the **Clear status message after** list, set the duration of your message.

You can augment your status with an optional status message.

5. Select **Done**.

> ✓ **TIP** In the web and desktop apps, you can also set your status from the Search box at the top of the window. Type one of the following commands, followed by **Enter** or **Return**: /available, /away, /brb, /busy, /dnd, or /offline.

Leave a team

You might find that you join a team and then realize that the team isn't useful to you, is inappropriate for your needs, or requires too much effort. Similarly, a team owner might add you to a team that you have no interest in. Whatever the scenario, remaining with a team you no longer require can result in unneeded notifications, unwanted messages, and unnecessary clutter in the Teams section of the app. You can eliminate all these problems by leaving any team you no longer need.

> **SEE ALSO** If you don't want to leave a team that you no longer participate in, you can hide it. For information about hiding teams, see "Modify a team" in Chapter 2, "Set up a team."

To leave a team

1. Tap **Teams** in the app bar.

2. Select **More options** (...) to the right of the team you want to leave.

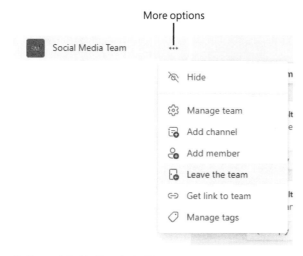

Options related to the selected team

3. Select **Leave the team**. Teams asks you to confirm.

4. Select **Leave the team** a second time. Teams removes you from the team.

Key points

- Microsoft Teams is a platform for communicating and collaborating with colleagues, peers, friends, and family.

- With Teams, you can have chat or channel conversations, participate in video meetings, place voice calls, and share files.

- You can use Teams on the web, on a PC or Mac, or on a mobile device.

- The three types of Teams apps—web, desktop, and mobile—share many of the same features, including the app bar, the Settings and more icon, and the Teams account profile button.

- You should change the default Teams profile picture (your initials) to a proper photo of yourself as soon as you can.

- You can join a team by using either a team code or a team link.

- Get into the habit of setting your status when you'll be away from your desk or when you don't want to be disturbed for a while.

- You can easily leave any team that you no longer find useful or relevant.

Set up a team

When your Teams administrator sets up your organization's Teams environment, an initial team is usually created automatically. This so-called *org-wide* team includes everyone in your organization. Many Teams organizations use only that initial team, modifying it as needed with new channels for different company purposes.

That one-team-only approach works well for small organizations and for organizations where it's reasonable for all the employees to have access to everything that happens with that single team. However, it's much more common to set up a team for each major company segment (such as a building, department, or floor), major company activity (such as a project or event), or major company group (such as a working group or task force). Anyone with Teams admin privileges in a Microsoft 365 environment can create a team, and the process usually takes just a few steps.

This chapter guides you through procedures related to creating a team from scratch, from one of your organization's predefined team templates, and from an existing team or Microsoft 365 group. You also learn how to add team members from within your organization and team guests from outside of your organization. Finally, you learn how to manage your team, including how to manage users and customize team settings.

In this chapter

- Create a team
- Manage your team's members and guests
- Manage your team

Create a team

If you have an idea for collaboration—whether it's an upcoming event, an ongoing project, or a collection of people with a common interest—and you decide that your organization's default team (if it has one) is too general or too large for your needs, you can create a new team. As long as you have a business or enterprise Teams account and you're either a Teams admin or your admin has given you team-creation permission, you can create as many teams as you need. You automatically become the owner of each team you create. A Teams admin can also create a team and designate one or more users as the team owners.

Each person in a team is assigned certain default permissions that determine the types of activities each person can perform within the team. These team permissions are based on each person's role within the team, and currently there are three roles available:

- **Team Owner**   The person who creates the team.
- **Team Member**   A person within the same organization as the team owner.
- **Guest**   A person outside of the organization of the team owner.

Do you *really* need to create a new team?

It's great that Teams enables you to set up a new team with just a few steps, but that low barrier to entry has a downside: It's far too easy to end up with too many teams! Teams is easy and intuitive to use, but every team extracts a certain cost from its members: exchanging chat messages, participating in channel conversations, sharing files, attending meetings, making and receiving calls, working with apps, and more. These costs aren't onerous if you're a member of just a few teams, but they can take over your entire day if you're a member of a few dozen teams.

Therefore, you should think twice (or even three times) before you add yet another team to your organization. To help you decide whether to create a new team, here are some questions to consider:

- What is the purpose of the team? You need to be clear about what you want your new team to achieve.

- Does that purpose justify an entirely new team? Planning the staff picnic might be worth a new team but planning the acknowledgment of Bob from Accounting's birthday is almost certainly not.

- Is there an existing team that can accomplish the same purpose? If your team's purpose is a subset of the mandate of an existing team, why reinvent the wheel?

- Are the potential members of your new team the same as the members of an existing team? If so, then it almost always makes more sense to modify the existing team to include the tasks you'd have assigned to the new team.

- Would a new channel within an existing team be enough to accomplish your purpose? If your new team's purpose is aligned with that of an existing team and your potential members are also included in the existing team, then strongly consider a new channel instead.

- Are the potential members of your new team already members of many existing teams? If so, then do you really want to burden those users with yet another team to follow?

- If the underlying reason for the new team is an event or project, is the duration of that event or project long enough to justify a new team? Long-term (meaning weeks, months, or even years) events or projects are usually team-worthy, but short-term (meaning days, hours, or even minutes) events or projects are usually not.

It's almost always a good idea to also talk with the potential members of your new team to see if they think it's a good idea or if what you're looking to accomplish can be done within the structure of an existing team.

> ⚠ **IMPORTANT** Your Microsoft Teams administrator must enable guest access before you can add guest users to your teams. The Teams default is to allow guest access, but your administrator might have disabled guest access.

> 🔍 **SEE ALSO** If you're a Teams admin, see "Add and manage users" in Chapter 14, "Administer Teams," to learn how to enable and disable guest access.

> ✅ **TIP** If you own a team with many members, administering that team can be quite a bit of work. To help, Teams enables you to designate specified team members as team owners to share the burden. Most large teams have at least two or three owners.

The following table lists several common Teams tasks and shows you which roles have permission to perform those tasks.

Task	Team Owner	Team Member	Guest
Create a channel	✓	✓	✓
Share a channel file	✓	✓	✓
Upload or download a file	✓	✓	✓
Participate in a channel conversation	✓	✓	✓
Participate in a private chat	✓	✓	✓
Get channel email	✓	✓	✓
Follow a channel	✓	✓	✓
Favorite a channel	✓	✓	✓
Delete or edit posted messages	✓	✓	✓
Share a chat file	✓	✓	
Edit or delete a channel	✓	✓	
Add apps (tabs, bots, or connectors)	✓	✓	
Discover and join public teams	✓	✓	
Allow @team or @[team name] mentions	✓	✓	

Task	Team Owner	Team Member	Guest
Allow @channel or @[channel name] mentions	✓	✓	
Add or remove members and guests	✓		
Assign owner role to members	✓		
Approve or reject requests to join the team	✓		
Set team permissions for channels, tabs, and connectors	✓		
Change the team picture	✓		
Renew a team	✓		
Archive or restore a team	✓		
Edit or delete a team	✓		
Allow usage of emojis, GIFs, and memes	✓		
Automatically show channels for the whole team	✓		
Choose who can manage tags	✓		

Teams gives you three ways to create a team:

- **From scratch** You specify all the details of the new team manually, including the type of team and the initial team members.

- **From a template** You create a team based on a *template*, which is a predefined team structure. Most templates come with multiple predefined channels, apps, and settings. For example, the Manage an Event template comes with the following channels: General, Announcements, Budget, Content, Logistics, Planning, and Marketing and PR. It also comes with several apps, including Wiki, Website, Tasks, and OneNote.

- **From an existing team or group** You create a new team where the members come from an existing Microsoft 365 group or from an existing team.

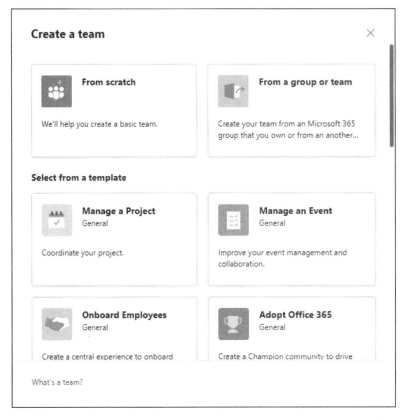

You can create a team from scratch, from a group or existing team, or from a template.

Teams enables you to create three kinds of teams:

- **Private** Creates a team that only people who receive an invitation can join and that only the team members can see in the Teams app.

- **Public** Creates a team that anyone can join and that everyone in the organization can see in the Teams app.

- **Org-wide** Creates a team that automatically includes everyone in your organization. No one is allowed to leave the team, and the team membership is maintained automatically as user accounts are added or deleted. Only a Teams administrator can create an org-wide team.

> ⚠ **IMPORTANT** As of this writing, org-wide teams are limited to organizations that have 10,000 users or less, and no organization can have more than five such teams.

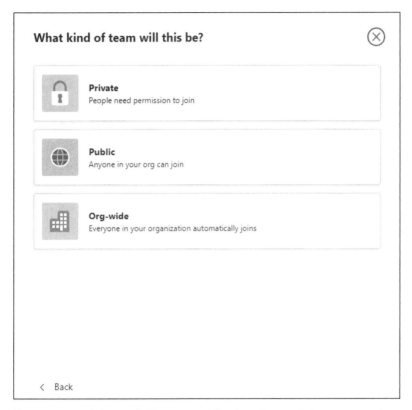

You can create a Private or Public team, and if you're a Teams admin, you can create an Org-wide team.

To set up a team from scratch in the web app or desktop app

1. In the app bar, select **Teams**.

2. At the bottom of the Teams panel, select **Join or create a team**.

3. On the **Join or create a team** page, point to the **Create a team** box, and then select the **Create team** button that appears.

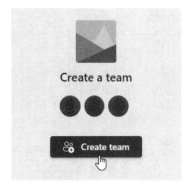

The button appears when you point to the box.

4. In the **Create a team** dialog, select **From scratch**.

5. Select the type of team you want to create: **Private**, **Public**, or **Org-wide** (you only see the **Org-wide** option if you're a Teams admin).

6. Enter a name that uniquely identifies the team.

7. Enter a description of the team to help people find it or to help members understand its purpose.

8. Select **Create**. Teams creates the team and prompts you to add members to it.

9. Do any of the following:

   - Start typing the name of the user you want to add, then click the user when that person's name appears. Repeat for each user you want to add.

   - Start typing the name of the distribution list or security group that you want to add, and then click the name of the list or group when it appears. Repeat for each list or group you want to add.

   - Type the email address of a person outside your organization, then select **Add** *address* **as a guest**, where *address* is the email address you typed.

   - If you don't want to add members now, select **Skip** and refer to the instructions given later in the "Manage your team's members and guests" section.

10. Select **Add**. Teams lists the members and guests.

11. If you want to designate a team member as a team owner, select the member's dropdown list and then select **Owner**.

12. Select **Close**. Teams sends notifications to each member and emails to each guest.

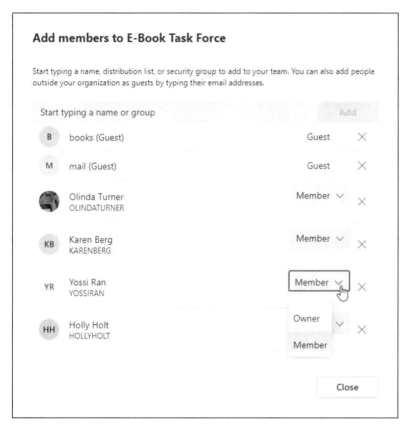

You can designate a team member as a team owner.

To set up a team from scratch using the Teams mobile app

1. In the app bar, tap **Teams**.

2. Do either of the following:

   - In the Android Teams app, tap **More** (the three vertical dots in the top-right corner) and then tap **Create new team**.

   - In the iOS or iPadOS Teams app, tap + and then tap **Create a team**.

3. Enter a name that uniquely identifies the team.

4. Enter a description of the team to help people find it or to help members understand its purpose.

5. Tap **Privacy**, tap the type of team you want to create (**Private** or **Public**), and then tap **Back** (<).

 TIP The mobile apps don't include the option to create an Org-Wide team.

6. Tap **Done**. Teams creates the team and prompts you to add members to your team.

7. Do any of the following:

   - Start typing the name of the user you want to add, and then tap the user when that person's name appears. Repeat for each user you want to add.

   - Start typing the name of the distribution list or security group that you want to add, and then tap the name of the list or group when it appears. Repeat for each list or group you want to add.

   - Type the email address of a person outside your organization, and then tap **Add** *address* **as a guest**, where *address* is the email address you typed.

   - If you don't want to add members now, tap **Skip** and refer to the instructions given later in the "Manage your team's members and guests" section.

8. Select **Add**. Teams sends notifications to each member and emails to each guest.

To set up a team from a template

1. In the Teams web app or desktop app, select **Teams** in the app bar.

2. At the bottom of the Teams panel, select **Join or create a team**.

3. In the **Create a team** box, select **Create team**.

4. In the **Select from a template** section of the **Create a team** dialog, select the template you want to use as the basis for your team. Teams displays lists of the channels and apps that come with the template's team structure.

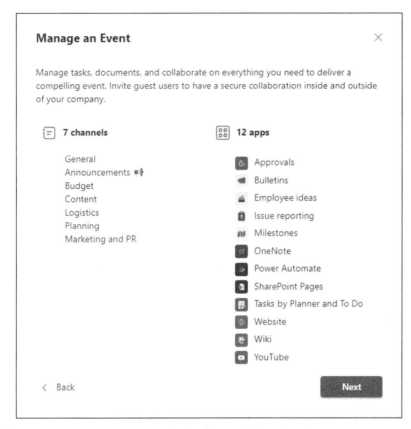

Each template comes with a predefined collection of channels and apps.

5. Select **Next**.

6. Select the type of team you want to create: **Private** or **Public**.

7. Type a name for your team.

8. Type a description for your team.

9. (Optional) If you want to rename any of the channels that come with the template (except the General channel, which can't be renamed), select **Customize channels** and then edit the channel names as needed.

10. Select **Create**. Teams creates the team, which might take several minutes. When the team is ready, Teams prompts you to add members to your team.

11. Do any of the following:

    - Start typing the name of the user you want to add, and then click the user when that person's name appears. Repeat for each user you want to add.

    - Start typing the name of the distribution list or security group that you want to add, and then click the name of the list or group when it appears. Repeat for each list or group you want to add.

    - Type the email address of a person outside your organization, and then select **Add** *address* **as a guest**, where *address* is the email address you typed.

    - If you don't want to add members now, select **Skip** and refer to the instructions given later in the "Manage your team's members and guests" section.

12. Select **Add**. Teams lists the members and guests.

13. If you want to designate a team member as a team owner, select the member's dropdown list and then select **Owner**.

14. Select **Close**. Teams sends notifications to each member and emails to each guest.

To set up a team from an existing team or group

1. In the Teams web app or desktop app, select **Teams** in the app bar.

2. At the bottom of the Teams panel, select **Join or create a team**.

3. In the **Create a team** box, select **Create team**.

4. In the **Create a team** dialog, select **From a group or team**.

5. If you want to base your new team on an existing team, select **Team** and continue with Step 6; otherwise, select **Microsoft 365 group**, select the group you want to use, select **Create**, and then skip the rest of these steps.

6. Type a name and description for the new team, choose **Private** or **Public**, select the checkbox for each item you want to include in the new team, and then select **Create**. Teams creates the team and prompts you to add members.

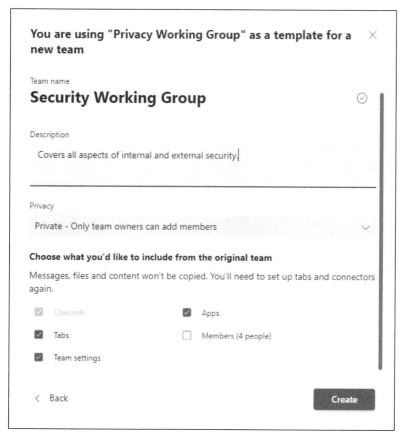

2

You can set up a new team from an existing one.

7. Do any of the following:

- Start typing the name of the user you want to add, and then click the user when that person's name appears. Repeat for each user you want to add.

- Start typing the name of the distribution list or security group that you want to add, and then click the name of the list or group when it appears. Repeat for each list or group you want to add.

- Type the email address of a person outside your organization, and then select **Add** *address* **as a guest**, where *address* is the email address you typed.

- If you don't want to add members now, select **Skip** and refer to the instructions given later in the "Manage your team's members and guests" section.

8. Select **Add**. Teams lists the members and guests.

9. If you want to designate a team member as a team owner, select the member's dropdown list and then select **Owner**.

10. Select **Close**. Teams sends notifications to each member and emails to each guest.

Manage your team's members and guests

In most cases, immediately after you create a team, you're prompted to add one or more members. (The exception is when you create a team from an existing Microsoft 365 group, which automatically adds the group's members to the team.) If you skipped adding members, or if you want to add more members after you create the team, you can use the team's management interface to add members or guests. You can also use a team's management interface to change a member's role (from Member to Owner or from Owner to Member) and to remove members and guests from the team.

Another useful team management feature is the tag. A *tag* is word or phrase that you use to categorize a subset of the people in your team based on some attribute they have in common. For example, you could tag people based on their department, job title, or location. You could also tag people based on their role within the team, the main skill they bring to the team, the team subgroup they belong to, and so on.

Why go to all this trouble? Because tags make it easy to communicate with different subsets of your team. For example, suppose your team has five members who work on app development. To notify those people about a channel or chat message, you'd have to @mention each person individually, which is cumbersome. If instead, you create an "App Development" tag and apply it to all five group members, you can add an @mention for the tag, and Teams will send a notification about your message to those five people.

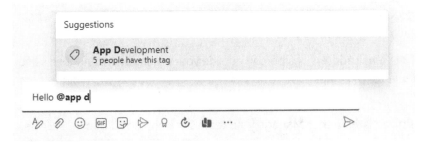

@mention a tag in a conversation to send the message to everyone associated with the tag.

To add members or guests to a team

1. In the Teams panel, to the right of the team name, select **More options (…)**, and then select **Add member**.

2. In the **Add members** dialog, do any of the following:

   - Start typing the name of the user you want to add, and then click the user when that person's name appears. Repeat for each user you want to add.

   - Start typing the name of the distribution list or security group that you want to add, and then click the name of the list or group when it appears. Repeat for each list or group you want to add.

   - Type the email address of a person outside your organization, and then select *user* **(Guest)**, where *user* is the username portion of the email address you typed.

3. Select **Add**. Teams lists the members and guests.

4. If you want to designate a team member as a team owner, select the member's dropdown list and then select **Owner**.

5. Select **Close**. Teams sends notifications to each member and emails to each guest.

To change a member's or owner's role

1. In the Teams panel, to the right of the team name, select **More options (…)** and then select **Manage team**.

2. On the **Members** page, select **Members and guests** to display the list of team's owners, members, and guests.

3. To the right of the owner's or member's name, expand the **Role** dropdown list, and then select either **Member** or **Owner**.

To create a tag and apply it to members or guests

1. In the Teams panel, to the right of the team name, select **More options (…)** and then select **Manage tags**.

2. On the **Tags** tab, select **Create tag**.

3. In the Create a new tag dialog, do the following:

- Enter a tag name of up to 40 characters.

- Type a tag description.

- Start typing the name of a member you want to add to the tag, and then select the member when that person's name appears. Repeat for each member you want to add to the tag.

- Select **Create**. Teams creates the tag and applies it to the members you selected.

Type a tag name and description and select the members you want to add to the tag.

To remove a member or guest

1. In the Teams panel, to the right of the team name, select **More options** (...), and then select **Manage team**.

2. On the **Members** page, select **Members and guests** to display the list of the team's members and guests.

3. Select **Remove** (**X**) to the right of the member or guest you want to remove. Teams removes the member or guest from the team.

Select Remove (X) to the right of the member or guest you want to remove.

Manage your team

Although it takes only a few steps to create a team, as the team owner, your responsibilities are only just beginning. There are quite a few team management tasks that are part of the day-to-day experience of owning a team. And the larger the team, the greater the management responsibility of owning the team. Ideally, for your larger teams, you've designated one or two members as team co-owners to share the managerial load.

Generate a team code or link

You can populate your team with members and guests either when you create the team or by using the team's management interface. In these cases, Teams adds the members and guests automatically and sends each person a notification (in Teams for members or via email for guests). Rather than automatically adding members, you might prefer to invite one or more people to your team and let them decide whether they want to join.

Teams offers two methods for sending an invitation to join a team:

- **Team code**   A seven-character code that a potential member can type into the Join a team with a code box (displayed by selecting the **Join or create a team** link in the Teams panel). Whether your team is public or private, a user who joins with a code is automatically added to the team.

Type a team code into the Join a team with a code box.

- **Team link**   A web address that a potential member can copy and paste into a web browser. The browser then opens the Teams app, which attempts to join the team. If your team is public, a user who joins with a link is automatically added to the team; if your team is private, you'll receive a join request that you can approve (or deny if the request came from someone you don't know or don't want on your team).

You can distribute team codes or links in any way that makes sense for you and for the people you want to invite, such as via email, text message, or social media. In Teams, you can distribute a team code or link via a chat or channel conversation.

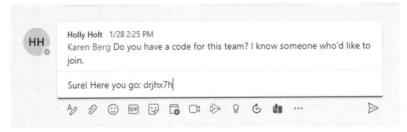

You can distribute a team code or link via email, text, social media, chat, or channel conversation.

To display the Settings page for a team

1. In the app bar, select **Teams**.

2. To the right of the team name, select **More options** (...), and then select **Manage team** to open the team's management interface with the Members tab selected.

3. Select the **Settings** tab.

To generate a team code

1. Display the **Settings** page for the team.

2. Select **Team code**. Teams generates a seven-character code for the team.

3. Select **Copy** and then distribute the code as needed.

Select Team code in the Settings tab to generate a code for your team.

To generate a team link

1. In the Teams panel, to the right of the team name, select **More options** (...), and then select **Get link to team**. Teams generates the link and displays it.

2. Select **Copy** and then distribute the link as needed.

Select Get a link to the team to generate a link for your team.

To accept or deny join requests

1. In the Teams panel, to the right of the team name, select **More options** (...), and then select **Manage team**.

2. Select the **Pending Requests** tab.

3. To add a person to the team, select that person's **Accept** button; otherwise, select that person's **Deny** button.

4. Do either of the following:

   - Repeat Step 5 as needed to handle all your pending requests.

   - Select either **Accept all** or **Deny all** if you have a lot of requests and you want to handle them all the same way.

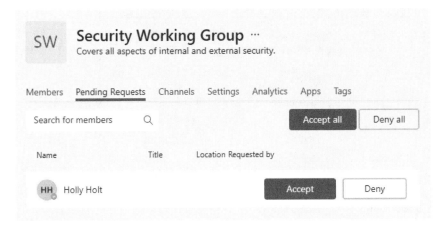

Select Accept to add the requester to your team or Deny to turn down the request.

Modify a team

Your team management duties might also require you to make modifications to your team. These modifications can include changing the team name, editing (or adding) its description, and changing the team type (Private, Public, or Org-wide).

2

Teams also gives you several ways to manage the list of teams in the Teams section of the app:

- **Hide a team** If you have a long list of teams and there's a team you don't follow or participate in often, you can hide the team. When you hide at least one team, Teams creates a **Hidden teams** section of the Teams panel and moves the hidden team there. To access a hidden team, you select **Hidden teams** and then select the team. If you later decide you no longer need the team to be hidden, you can show it again.

- **Archive a team** If you have a team that's no longer active but still contains valuable content, you can archive that team. To *archive* a team means that all the team's content becomes read-only and can't be changed. The team is also hidden. If needed, however, you can still add or remove members and change member roles. You can also still access and search the content. If you later decide you no longer need the team to be archived, you can restore it.

- **Delete a team** If you have a team that you no longer need and that contains no content that you want to archive, you can delete the team to reduce clutter in the Teams panel.

To edit a team's name, description, or type

1. To the right of the team name in the Teams panel, select **More options** (...), and then select **Edit team**.
2. Edit the team name.
3. Edit the team description.
4. In the **Privacy** list, select a new team type: **Private**, **Public**, or **Org-wide**.
5. Select **Done**. Teams updates the team info.

To hide a team

- To the right of the team name in the Teams panel, select **More options** (...), and then select **Hide**. Teams moves the team to the **Hidden teams** section.

To show a hidden team

1. At the end of the list of teams in the Teams panel, select **Hidden teams**.
2. To the right of the team name, select **More options** (...), and then select **Show**. Teams unhides the team.

To archive a team

1. In the app bar, select **Teams**.

2. In the lower-right corner of the Teams panel, select **Manage teams**.

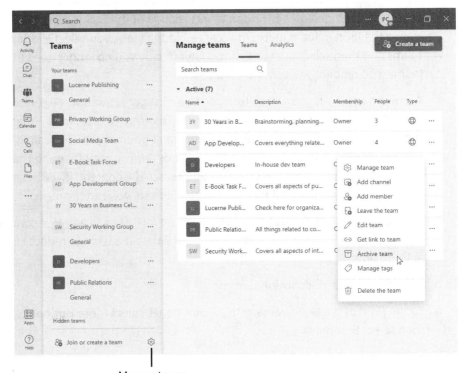

Manage teams

Archive teams from the Manage teams page.

3. On the **Manage teams** page, to the right of the team name, select **More options (...)**, and then select **Archive team**. Teams asks you to confirm.

4. In the **Want to archive "*Team Name*"** dialog, do one or both of the following:

   - If you believe team members might still try to modify the team content using the team's associated SharePoint site, select the **Make the SharePoint site read-only for team members** checkbox.

   - Select **Archive**. Teams archives and hides the team.

To restore an archived team

1. In the app bar, select **Teams**.

2. In the lower-right corner of the Teams panel, select **Manage teams**.

3. On the **Manage teams** page, select the **Archived** section heading to display the list of archived teams.

4. To the right of the team you want to restore, select **More options** (...), and then select **Restore team**. Teams restores the team but leaves the team hidden.

5. In the Teams panel, at the end of the list of teams, select **Hidden teams**.

6. To the right of the team name, select **More options** (...), and then select **Show**. Teams unhides the team.

To delete a team

1. In the Teams panel, to the right of the team name, select **More options** (...), and then select **Delete the team**. Teams asks you to confirm.

2. Select the **I understand that everything will be deleted** checkbox.

3. Select **Delete team**. Teams deletes the team.

Customize team settings

Unless you use an existing team as the basis of a new team, each team you create comes with a collection of default settings. These settings fall into the following seven categories:

- **Team picture** Customize the team avatar with a photo or other artwork.

- **Member permissions** Set the specific permissions given to team members. These permissions determine whether each member can perform specific tasks, such as create and update channels; delete and restore channels; add and remove apps; create and remove tabs; and delete and edit their own messages.

- **Guest permissions** Set the specific permissions given to team guests. These permissions determine whether guests can create and update channels and whether guests can delete channels.

- **@mentions**   Determine whether team members can use @team, @[*team name*], @channel, and @[*channel name*] mentions. @team and @[*team name*] mentions notify every person on the team, while @channel and @[*channel name*] mentions notify everyone in the current channel or the specified channel name, respectively.

- **Team code**   Generate a team code (see "Generate a team code or link" earlier in this chapter).

- **Fun stuff**   Determine whether team members can use animated GIFs, stickers, memes, and custom memes.

- **Tags**   Determine which team roles can manage tags: team owners only or both team owners and team members.

To customize the team picture

1. Display the **Settings** page for the team.

2. Expand the **Team picture** section and select **Change picture**.

3. In the **Change picture** dialog, select **Upload picture**.

4. In the **Open** dialog, select the image file you want to use for the picture, and then select **Open**.

5. In the **Change picture** dialog, select **Save** to update the team picture.

To customize the team member permissions

1. Display the **Settings** page for the team.

2. Expand the **Member permissions** section.

3. Clear the checkbox for each permission you want to disallow to members.

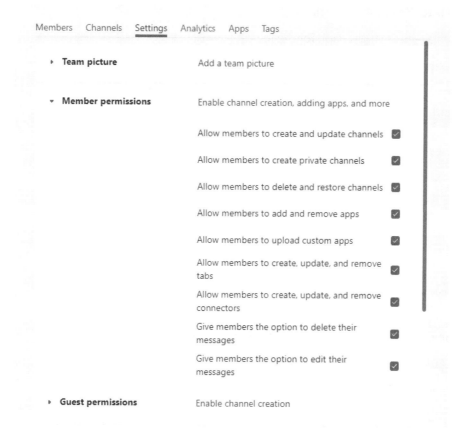

In the Settings tab, select Member permissions to customize the permissions given to each team member.

To customize the team guest permissions

1. Display the **Settings** page for the team.

2. Expand the **Guest permissions** section.

3. For each permission you want to allow to guests, select the checkbox.

▾ **Guest permissions**	Enable channel creation
	Allow guests to create and update channels ☐
	Allow guests to delete channels ☐

In the Settings tab, select Guest permissions to customize the permissions given to each team guest.

To customize the team @mentions

1. Display the **Settings** page for the team.

2. Expand the **@mentions** section.

3. For each type of @mention you want to disallow to members, clear the checkbox.

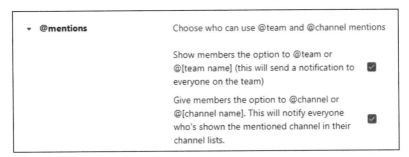

In the Settings tab, select @mentions to customize who can use @team and @channel mentions.

To customize the usage of animated GIFs, stickers, and memes

1. Display the **Settings** page for the team.

2. Expand the **Fun stuff** section.

3. If you don't want team members to post animated GIFs, clear the **Giphy** checkbox.

4. If you leave the **Giphy** checkbox selected, use the dropdown list to select a filter setting for inappropriate content: **Moderate** or **Strict**.

5. If you don't want team members to post stickers and memes, clear the **Stickers and memes** checkbox. Teams also clears and hides the **Custom Memes** checkbox.

6. If you leave the **Stickers and memes** checkbox selected, but you don't want team members to upload their own memes, clear the **Custom Memes** checkbox.

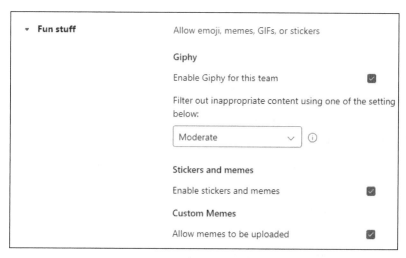

2

In the Settings tab, select Fun stuff to customize whether members can use animated GIFs, stickers, and memes.

To customize who can manage tags

1. Display the **Settings** page for the team.

2. Expand the **Tags** section.

3. In the **Tags are managed by** dropdown list, select **Team owners** or **Team owners and members** to specify who can manage tags.

4. Turn off the toggle beside each app that you don't want to automatically apply tags.

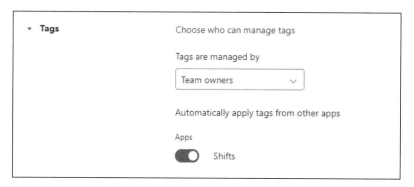

In the Settings tab, select Tags to customize who can manage tags in your team.

Key points

- Only create a new team if the team's purpose can't be fulfilled by an existing team.

- Each person in a team has one of three roles: owner, member, or guest. These roles define the permissions available to each person within the team. Specific permissions are controlled by the Teams administrator for your organization.

- When you create a team, you're automatically assigned the owner role.

- You can create a new team from scratch, from a template, from an existing team, or from an existing Microsoft 365 group.

- There are three kinds of teams: private (invitation-only), public (anyone can join), and org-wide (includes everyone in your organization). Only Teams administrators can create org-wide teams.

- Assign tags to team members based on attributes such as job title or department, and then message all those members by using an @mention of the tag.

- To invite someone to join your private team, send them a team code or team link.

- If you rarely use a team, hide it; if a team is inactive but you still want its content available, archive it; if a team is no longer viable and you don't need its content, delete it.

Work with channels

Channels are one of the most useful and most important Teams concepts because it's only through judicious use of channels that you avoid your team descending into an inefficient, frustrating, and chaotic mess. That's because you use channels to break up a team into manageable chunks, where each chunk—that is, each channel—represents a subtopic of the overall team topic. By structuring a team with multiple channels, you keep conversations, files, apps, and app notifications separated and organized by the channel subtopics.

A channel, then, is a bit like a subfolder in a file system. You could organize your desktop computer by storing all your data in a single folder, but it's much more efficient to create subfolders to separate and work with related data.

This chapter guides you through procedures related to creating both standard and private channels and adding people to those channels. You also learn how to work with channel properties and share a channel. Finally, you learn how to follow a channel, pin a channel to the top of the channel list, silence and hide channels, and leave channels you no longer use.

In this chapter

- Create a channel
- Manage a channel
- Work with channels

Create a channel

A channel is a major element of a team's structure because it enables a subset of the team's activities and content to exist in a separate workspace. When you create a team, it comes with a default General channel that can't be hidden or deleted. The General channel is useful for conversations, files, and apps that apply to the entire team. However, it's a rare team that can operate efficiently with only the General channel. Most teams will require several extra channels. Here are some example teams and the types of channels they might require:

- **Company division**   You might want to set up a channel for each major subdivision within that division. For example, a company's North American division might have subdivisions for Canada, Mexico, and the United States, each of which could have its own channel.

- **Department**   You might want separate channels for each office or function within the department. For example, a Finance department team might need channels for Accounting, Accounts Receivable, Accounts Payable, and Payroll.

- **Upcoming event**   You might want separate channels for event-related planning, budgeting, logistics, content, and marketing.

- **Project**   You might want separate channels for project-related planning, resources, and announcements.

- **Sports team**   You might want separate channels for coaches, players, and training.

If you decide that your team needs channels beyond its default General channel, then you or anyone else on the team can create those channels in just a few steps.

When you create a channel, you can apply one of the following two privacy options:

- **Standard**   Everyone who is part of the team has access to the channel. Select this option for most of your channels.

- **Private**   Only specified members and guests have access to the channel. Select this option if a channel has content or value for only certain people on your team or if the channel contains sensitive information that's not suitable for all team members.

Should you create a channel?

Channels are so useful and such an important element of the Teams experience that Microsoft made it easy for team owners, team members, and even team guests to create new channels. Allowing everyone on a team to add channels is very democratic and very empowering, but it's also very dangerous. Why? Because if you give people the power to perform some task, a certain percentage of those people will wield that power just for the sake of wielding it. That is, instead of determining in advance whether there is a solid and compelling need for a channel, some team members will just go ahead and create the channel. The result? They end up creating a team with dozens of channels, many of them focused either on extremely niche topics or even on nothing at all!

A team with an excessive number of channels is difficult to follow and makes it tough for members to stay current with the latest developments. Therefore, if you have an idea for a new team channel, think about whether your channel will really add value to the team. How many people on the team will really be interested in the channel's topic? Is there an existing channel that's a good fit for your topic? Use the Team's General channel to start a new conversation about your proposed channel and solicit feedback from team owners and members. If you get lots of positive feedback, go ahead and create the new channel. If, on the other hand, you run up against significant resistance to the idea, then it's time to shelve it and move on.

3

The channels you add to a team appear in the Teams panel as a nested list under each team name. If you don't see a team's channels, select the team name to expand the list of its channels. Select the team name again to collapse the channel list.

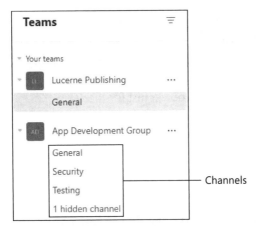

Channels

In the Teams panel, select a team to view its list of channels.

Note that although team owners always see all the available channels, by default team members don't necessarily see all of a team's channels:

- If a team has three or fewer standard channels, team members see all the channels.

- If a team has four or more standard channels, team members see the General channel and the first two standard channels that were added to the team. All other standard channels are hidden by default and must be accessed by selecting the *x* **hidden channel(s)** link in the channel list (where *x* is the number of hidden channels). If needed, team members can unhide any of these channels.

- When you create a standard channel, you can ensure that the new channel is not hidden by default by selecting the **Automatically show this channel in everyone's channel list** checkbox.

- For a private channel, members who have access always see the channel, while members without access never see the channel.

As with a team, the person who creates a channel is the channel owner. Channel owners have several permissions that channel members don't have. These permissions include the following:

- Adding new members to a private channel
- Changing user roles
- Removing channel members and guests
- Editing the channel's name and description
- Modifying channel settings
- Deleting the channel

If you find as a channel owner that you want to share or delegate some of these tasks, then you need to change the role of one or more channel participants from member to owner.

To create a standard channel

1. In the app bar, select **Teams**.

2. In the Teams panel, to the right of the team name, select **More options (...)**, and then select **Add channel**.

3. In the **Create a channel** dialog, do the following and then select **Add**:

   - In the **Channel name** text box, type a name for the channel.

   - (Optional) In the **Description** text box, type a description of the channel to help members understand its purpose.

   - In the **Privacy** dropdown list, select **Standard**.

   - If you want the channel to not be hidden in each team member's channel list, select the **Automatically show this channel in everyone's channel list** checkbox.

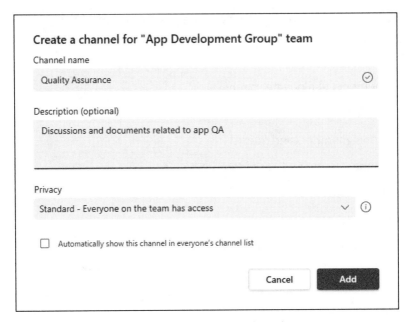

Using the Create a channel dialog to add a standard channel.

To create a private channel

1. In the Teams panel, to the right of the team name, select **More options** (...), and then select **Add channel**.

2. In the **Create a Channel** dialog, do the following and then select **Create**:

   - In the **Channel name** text box, type a name for the channel.

   - (Optional) In the **Description** text box, type a description for the channel.

   - In the **Privacy** dropdown list, select **Private**.

3. In the **Add members** dialog, do the following to give members and guests access to the private channel:

   - To give a member access, start typing the member's name, and then select the member when that person's name appears. Repeat for each member you want to give access to the private channel.

- To give a guest access, type the guest's email address, and then select the guest when that person's email address appears. Repeat for each guest you want to give access to the private channel.

- If you don't want to give access to members and guests now, select **Skip** and refer to the instructions given later in the "To add members to a team's private channel" section.

4. Select **Add**. Teams lists the members and guests.

5. Select **Done**. Teams adds the private channel and denotes that it's private by displaying it with a lock icon. Teams also notifies the specified members and guests that they now have access to the private channel.

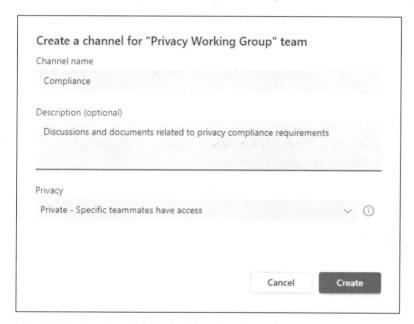

Using the Create a channel dialog to add a private channel.

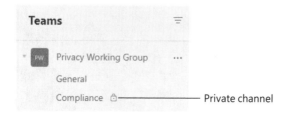

Private channels are denoted in the channel list with a lock icon

To add members to a team's private channel

1. In the Teams panel, to the right of the private channel name, select **More options (...)**, and then select **Add members**.

2. In the **Add members** dialog, do the following to give members and guests access to the private channel:

   - To give a member access, start typing the member's name, and then select the member when that person's name appears. Repeat for each member you want to give access to the private channel.

   - To give a guest access, type the guest's email address, and then select the guest when that person's email address appears. Repeat for each guest you want to give access to the private channel.

3. Select **Add**. Teams lists the members and guests.

4. Select **Close**. Teams notifies the added members and guests that they now have access to the private channel.

To change a member to an owner in a private channel

1. In the Teams panel, to the right of the private channel name, select **More options (...)**, and then select **Manage channel**.

2. On the **Members** tab, select **Members and guests** to display the list of the team's members and guests.

3. Select the member's dropdown list and then select **Owner**.

Manage a channel

Creating a channel isn't difficult, but it's just the beginning when it comes to the management duties you need to consider as the owner of that channel. As a general rule, the larger the channel (especially the General channel of a large team), the longer the list of management tasks that comes with being the channel owner. If you find these tasks onerous, consider designating one or more channel members as co-owners to share the managerial responsibilities.

3

The tasks involved in managing a channel generally fall into three categories:

- Editing and deleting channels
- Adding and configuring channel connectors
- Customizing channel settings

To edit a channel's name, description, or type

1. In the Teams panel, to the right of the channel name, select **More options (...)**, and then select **Edit this channel**.

2. Edit the channel name.

3. Edit the channel description.

4. Select **Save**. Teams updates the channel info.

To delete a channel

1. In the Teams panel, to the right of the channel name, select **More options (...)**, and then select **Delete this channel**. Teams asks you to confirm.

2. Select **Delete**.

Add and configure channel connectors

A *connector* is a communications link between your channel and a third-party service that enables the service to post messages to the channel. Here are some example connectors:

- **Forms**   Connects to Microsoft Forms and enables channel participants to create, interact with, and see the results of polls, surveys, and quizzes.

- **RSS**   Connects to an RSS (Really Simple Syndication) feed that displays the most recent posts to a blog or similar site.

- **AppReviewBot**   Connects to the Google Play Store or the iOS App Store to monitor app reviews.

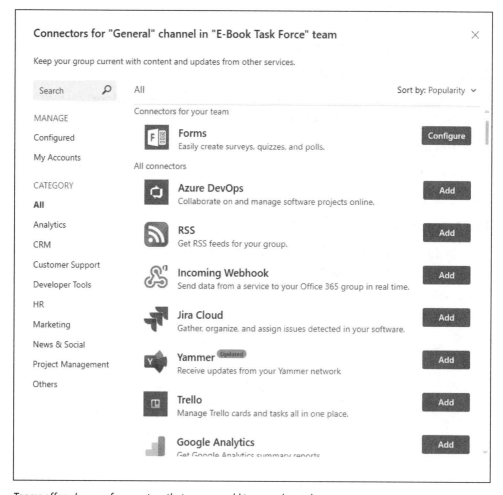

Teams offers dozens of connectors that you can add to your channels.

To work with connectors in a channel, you first add the connector to the channel, and then you configure the connector.

To add a connector

1. In the Teams panel, to the right of the channel name, select **More options (…)**, and then select **Connectors**.

2. In the **Connectors** dialog, select **Add** to the right of the connector you want to add to the channel. Teams displays a description of the connector.

3. Select **Add**. Teams adds the connector to the channel.

An example of a connector description page.

To configure an added connector

1. In the Teams panel, to the right of the channel name, select **More options** (**…**), and then select **Connectors**.

2. In the **Connectors** dialog, select **Configure** to the right of the connector you want to work with.

3. In the connector-specific dialog (the layout of which will vary depending on the connector), enter the connection name and specify the settings required by the connector.

4. Select **Save**.

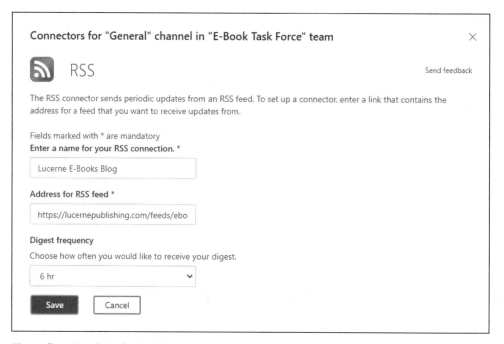

The configuration dialog for the RSS connector.

Customize channel settings

Each channel you create comes with one or more default settings. Only you as the owner of the channel (or any channel participant that you've given the Owner role) can modify these settings. The settings you work with depend on the channel:

- **General channel**   In the General channel that Teams creates automatically with each new team, there's just one setting that you use to determine who can post to the channel:

    - **Anyone can post messages**   This is the default setting, which enables all channel owners, members, and guests to post messages to the channel.

    - **Anyone can post; show alert that posting will notify everyone**
      All channel owners, members, and guests can post messages to the channel. However, Teams displays a message above the posting text box that specifies the number of people who will see the message. Since, by definition, the General channel includes everyone in the team, select this option for large teams to help prevent trivial or off-topic messages going out to the entire team.

      You can configure a General channel to display an alert that shows the number of people who will see the message.

    - **Only owners can post messages**   Select this option if you want to restrict channel posts to just channel owners. This is the setting you want if you prefer the General channel to show only team announcements or similar important messages.

■ **Standard channel** If you create a standard channel, the available settings relate to *channel moderation*, which is the capability to determine who can post new messages to the channel and what other channel members can do with those posts. There are two channel moderation possibilities. If Channel moderation is set to Off (the default setting), it means that you control who can post new messages to the channel by choosing one of the following options:

- **Everyone can start a new post** This is the default, and it means that all channel owners, members, and guests can post new messages to the channel.

- **Everyone except guests can start a new post** Select this option to restrict new channel posts to just channel owners and members.

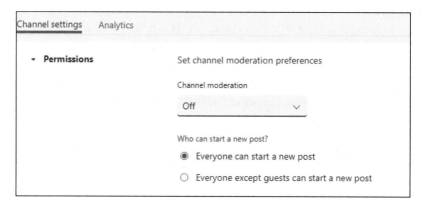

With channel moderation off, everyone can post new messages by default.

 TIP Channel moderation settings are available only for public channels other than the default General channel.

■ If Channel moderation is set to On, then only channel moderators can start new posts to the channel. By default, Teams designates the team owners as moderators of the channel, but you can add other moderators by selecting the Manage button. You use the following checkboxes (all selected by default) to control the permissions of the channel's non-moderators:

- **Allow members to reply to channel messages** Clear this checkbox to prevent non-moderators from replying to moderator posts.

- **Allow members to pin channel messages** Clear this checkbox to prevent non-moderators from pinning moderator posts.

- **Allow bots to submit channel messages** Clear this checkbox to prevent chatbots from posting messages to the channel. A *chatbot* (usually shortened to just *bot*) is an app feature that enables channel members to interact with the app by exchanging channel messages.

- **Allow connectors to submit channel messages** Clear this checkbox to prevent connectors from posting messages to the channel.

3

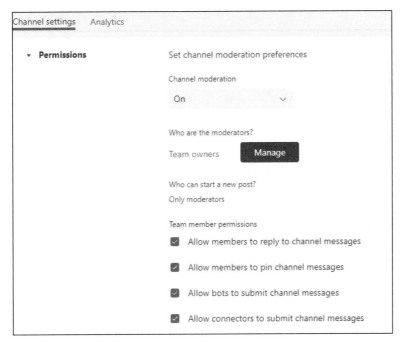

With channel moderation on, only moderators can post new messages.

- **Private channel** If you create a private channel, the available settings fall into three categories:

  - **Member permissions** Set the specific permissions given to team members. These permissions determine whether each member can perform specific tasks, such as create, update, and delete tabs, delete their own messages, and edit their own messages.

  - **@mentions** Determine whether team members can use @channel and @[*channel name*] mentions. @channel and @[*channel name*] mentions notify everyone in the current channel or the specified channel name, respectively.

  - **Fun stuff** Determine whether team members can use animated GIFs, stickers, memes, and custom memes.

To display the Channel Settings page for a channel

- In the Teams panel, to the right of the channel name, select **More options (...)**, and then select **Manage channel**.

To customize General channel permissions

1. Display the **Channel settings** page for the channel.

2. In the **Permissions** section, select the posting permission setting you want to apply to the channel.

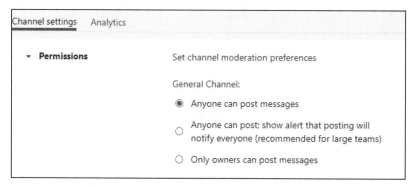

The General Channel setting determines who can post messages.

To configure posting permissions for an unmoderated channel

1. Display the **Channel settings** page for the channel.

2. In the **Channel moderation** list, select **Off**.

3. For the **Who can start a new post?** setting, select who can post new messages to the channel.

To configure posting permissions for a moderated channel

1. Display the **Channel settings** page for the channel.

2. In the **Channel moderation** list, select **On**.

3. To designate other channel moderators, select **Manage**. In the **Add or Remove Moderators** dialog, start typing the name of the team member you want to add as a moderator, and then select that person's name when it appears. Repeat to add as many moderators as you need, and then select **Done**.

4. In the **Team member permissions** section, clear the checkbox beside each permission you want to revoke.

To display the Settings page for a private channel

1. In the Teams panel, to the right of the channel name, select **More options** (...), and then select **Manage channel**.

2. In the channel's management interface, select the **Settings** tab.

To customize private channel member permissions

1. Display the **Settings** page for the private channel.

2. Expand the **Member permissions** section.

3. For each permission you want to disallow to members, clear the checkbox.

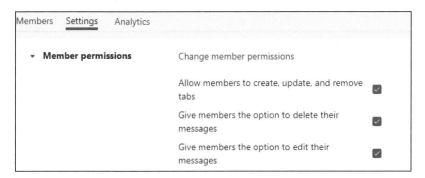

In the Settings tab, select Member permissions to customize the permissions given to each channel member.

To customize private channel @mentions

1. Display the **Settings** page for the private channel.

2. Expand the **@mentions** section.

3. Clear the checkbox to disallow @channel or @[*channel name*] mentions.

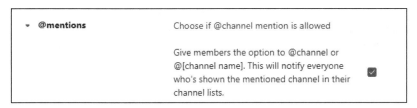

In the Settings tab, select @mentions to customize who can use @channel mentions.

To customize the usage of animated GIFs, stickers, and memes for a private channel

1. Display the **Settings** page for the private channel.

2. Expand the **Fun stuff** section.

3. If you don't want channel members to post animated GIFs, clear the **Giphy** checkbox.

4. If you leave the **Giphy** checkbox selected, use the dropdown list to select a filter setting for inappropriate content: **Moderate** or **Strict**.

5. If you don't want channel members to post stickers and memes, clear the **Stickers and memes** checkbox. Teams also clears and hides the **Custom Memes** checkbox.

6. If you leave the **Stickers and memes** checkbox selected, but you don't want channel members to upload their own memes, clear the **Custom Memes** checkbox.

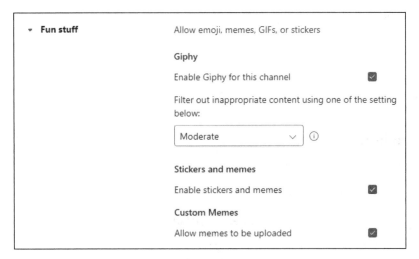

In the Settings tab, select Fun Stuff to customize whether channel members can use animated GIFs, stickers, and memes.

Work with channels

If you're a team member, Teams gives you quite a few ways to work with your channels, including the following:

- **Configure channel notifications** You can tailor the notifications you receive for each of your channels. For example, for channels that are important to you, you probably want to receive every possible notification; for less important channels, you might prefer to receive notifications only when someone mentions you. Teams supports three levels of channel notification:

  - **All activity** You see a notification for every post, every reply, and every channel and personal mention.

  - **Off** You only see a notification if someone replies directly to one of your channel posts or if someone mentions you in a post.

  - **Custom** Enables you to choose which notifications you want to receive.

  > ⚠ **IMPORTANT** Teams doesn't offer a command to mute all notifications for a channel. The best you can do is choose Off for the notification setting, which means you'll only get notified when someone mentions you or replies to one of your posts.

- **Pin a channel** If you're a member of many teams that have many channels, finding a specific channel can be time-consuming because you have to find the correct team, display its channels, and then select the channel you want. However, if you find that you spend most of your Teams time in just two or three channels, you can access those channels much faster by pinning them. To *pin* a channel is to move a copy of the channel to a special Pinned section at the top of the Teams panel.

3

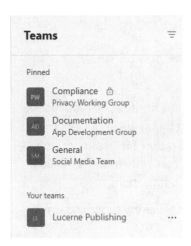

After you pin at least one channel, Teams adds a Pinned section to the top of the Teams panel.

- **Hide a channel**   If a team's channel list displays a channel you don't follow or participate in very much, you might want to hide the channel. When you hide at least one channel, Teams creates an *x* hidden channel(s) link (where *x* is the number of hidden channels) under the team's channel list and moves the hidden channel there. To access a hidden channel, you select *x* hidden channel(s) and then select the channel. If you later decide you no longer need the channel to be hidden, you can show it again.

- **Show a channel**   Teams sometimes hides channels automatically to avoid cluttering a team's channel list. If you frequently participate in one of these hidden channels, having to constantly select the *x* hidden channel(s) link is an extra step you don't need. Instead, you can ask Teams to show the channel.

- **Share a link to a channel**   If an interesting or useful discussion arises in a channel, you might want to let another channel member know about it. If you know that person is a member of a large number of teams and/or channels, you can make that person's life a bit easier by sending her a direct link to the channel. This saves her the trouble of finding the correct channel in the Teams panel. The person to whom you send the link must be a member or guest of that channel.

- **Leave a channel**   If you have a channel that you no longer want to follow, you can leave the channel to reduce clutter in the team's channel list.

To configure channel notifications

1. In the Teams panel, to the right of the channel name, select **More options (…)**, and then select **Channel notifications**.

2. Select the notification level you prefer: **All activity**, **Off**, or **Custom**.

3. If you select **Custom**, use the **Channel notification settings** dialog to configure the notifications you prefer, and then select **Save**.

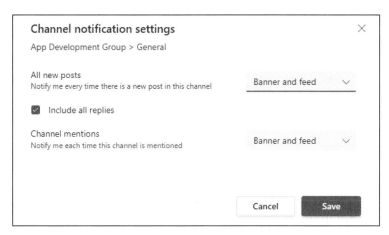

Use the Channel notification settings dialog to configure custom notifications for a channel.

To pin a channel

- In the Teams panel, to the right of the channel name, select **More options (…)**, and then select **Pin**.

To unpin a channel

- In the Teams panel, to the right of the channel name, select **More options (…)**, and then select **Unpin**.

To hide a channel

- In the Teams panel, to the right of the channel name, select **More options (…)**, and then select **Hide**. Teams moves the channel to the *x* **hidden channel(s)** section of the team.

To show a hidden channel

1. In the team's channel list, select *x* **hidden channel(s)** to display a menu of the team's hidden channels.

2. Select **Show** to the right of the channel you want to unhide.

To share a link to a channel

1. In the Teams panel, to the right of the channel name, select **More options (...)**, and then select **Get link to channel**.

2. In the **Get a link to the channel** dialog, select **Copy** to copy the link address to the Clipboard.

3. Paste the link into a message or post and then send it.

Select Get link to channel to generate a link for your channel.

To leave a channel

1. In the Teams panel, to the right of the channel name, select **More options (...)**, and then select **Leave the channel**. Teams asks you to confirm.

2. Select **Leave the channel**. Teams removes you as a member of the channel.

Key points

- A channel is a team structural element that enables a subset of the team's activities and content to exist in a separate workspace.

- Any team owner, member, or guest can create a channel.

- Each channel is either a standard channel, where everyone on the team has access, or a private channel, where only specified members and guests have access.

- A connector is a communications link between a channel and a third-party service that enables the service to post messages to the channel.

- Channel moderation is the capability to determine who can send new posts to the channel and what other channel members can do with those posts.

Converse in a channel

One of the great advantages of team channels is that they bring structure and relevancy to a team-related topic. The channel structure comes with the nature of the channel itself, which is organized into various tabs. For example, you deal with file-related tasks on the Files tab. The channel relevancy comes from the fact that, outside of the General channel that includes all team members, the users of a particular channel are members because they or someone else thought the channel topic to be of sufficient interest.

The inherent structure and relevancy of a channel are particularly important when it comes to messaging. Too much of what passes for communication these days consists of email or texts sent to large groups. These messages are either deleted or archived without much thought, and most of the recipients have no interest in the message. In a Teams channel, by contrast, all channel conversations are stored on the channel's Posts tab, and the distribution of each message is limited to the channel members.

This chapter guides you through procedures related to creating standard channel conversations, multichannel conversations, and channel announcements. You also learn how to enhance channel messages by formatting them, working with @mentions, and using emojis and reactions. Finally, you also learn several channel message management techniques, including how to save, delete, and share channel messages.

In this chapter

- Create a channel conversation
- Enhance channel messages
- Manage channel messages

Create a channel conversation

A channel conversation is a collection of related messages within a channel. Most conversations revolve around a particular subtopic of the channel. Every channel conversation appears within the channel's Posts tab.

 IMPORTANT Remember that channels are only available in the business and enterprise versions of Teams.

Note, too, that channel conversations are *threaded*, which means that each conversation consists of two main parts:

- **Original message**   The initial message that you or some other channel member posts to the channel.

- **Replies**   The messages that other people post in response to the original message.

When it comes to posting the original message, you can create four main types of channel conversations:

- **Simple conversation**   A threaded conversation over a single channel, with no subject line. Use this type of conversation for brief exchanges with channel members.

- **Conversation with a subject**   A threaded conversation over a single channel, with an overall subject line. Like a well-crafted subject line in an email message, a thoughtful subject line in a channel conversation identifies the conversation, summarizes the topic, and provides context for readers. Except for the most trivial exchanges, your channel conversations should include a subject.

- **Multichannel conversation**   A threaded conversation over two or more channels, with an optional subject line. Use this type of conversation if the topic of your thread is of interest to multiple channels in one or more teams.

- **Announcement**   A threaded conversation with a headline and a subhead. Use announcements only when you have important news to share. You can optionally post announcements to multiple channels.

On the reply side of the conversation, when you're posting an original message, you also get to decide who can reply to the message. You have two choices:

- **Everyone can reply**   This is the default, and it means that every channel member can post a reply both to your initial message and to any other message in the conversation thread.

- **You and moderators can reply**   The only people who can post replies in this thread are you and the channel's moderators.

4

 SEE ALSO For more information about channel moderators, see "Customize channel settings" in Chapter 3, "Work with channels."

Which method of communication should I use?

Before Microsoft Teams came along, we all had plenty of options to choose from when it came to communicating with others. We had email, of course, and text messages. We had regular phone calls and video phone calls. And we had the collaboration tools built into the desktop and online versions of Word, Excel, and other Office (now Microsoft 365) apps.

But now you're a member of a team, and that membership brings an entirely new set of communications tools: channel conversations, one-on-one chat, group chat, meetings, chat *within* a meeting, and Teams-based phone calls.

This all leaves you with an abundance of options when it comes to communicating with others. Which medium is the best (or easiest or most efficient) one to choose?

To help you answer that question, remember that the main point of Teams is to bring focus and organization to some subset of your work or personal life. The problem with email and text messages is that they require you and the people you correspond with to impose your own order on your communications. Sure, *you* might set up a subfolder in Outlook to store messages related to a particular topic, but you have no guarantee that everyone else has done the same. *You* might save pertinent text messages, but are your conversation partners doing the same? Who knows?

With Teams, you don't have to worry about any of that because your written communications are automatically stored within the context in which they were created. Looking for a chat message from a meeting? Open the Chat panel and find the meeting chat transcript. Looking for a channel conversation? Display that channel's Posts tab.

There's nothing wrong with regular email and text messaging, but Teams makes communication easier by making it more focused:

- When you want a quick discussion with someone in the same Teams organization, start a Teams chat with that person.

- When you want a quick discussion that involves multiple people in the same Teams organization, start a group chat.

- If you're in a Teams meeting and you want a quick discussion that involves something related to the meeting content or topic, start an in-meeting chat.

- When you want to start a more involved discussion that involves everyone in a particular team, create a new conversation in the team's General channel.

- When you want to talk about something that only relates to the topic of a particular channel, create a new conversation within that channel.

Most channel conversations take place in the channel's Posts tab, which includes a button for starting a new conversation. However, Teams also gives you two other methods for starting a channel conversation:

- **Via email**   A team owner can generate a unique email address for any channel. When someone sends an email message to that address, Teams posts the message as the original message in a new channel conversation. The subject line of the email becomes the subject of the channel conversation. The team owner can allow anyone to send emails to the channel address, or they can restrict sending to just team members or to just specified domain names.

A channel message sent to the channel's email address

> **IMPORTANT** Channel email messages can't have more than 20 file attachments or 50 inline images, and each attached file can be no bigger than 10 MB.

> **IMPORTANT** Channel email integration is controlled by your Teams administrator and might be disabled in your deployment. Check with your Teams admin.

> **SEE ALSO** If you're a Teams administrator, you can disable or customize channel email integration for your teams; see "Manage Teams via policies" in Chapter 13, "Administer Teams."

- **Via Outlook**   You can share an Outlook email message (including attachments, if any) to a specified team. Teams posts the message as the original message in a new channel conversation but without a subject line.

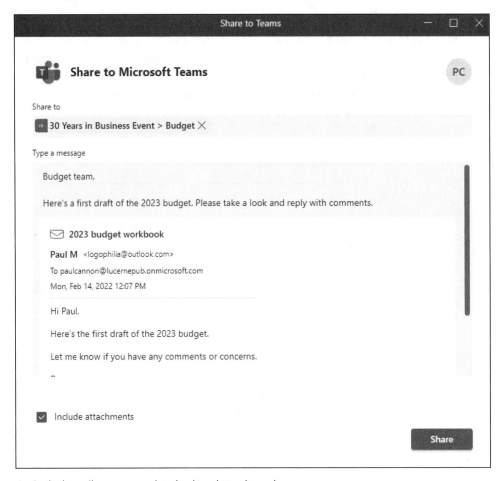

An Outlook email message ready to be shared to a channel

To create a simple channel conversation

1. In the Teams panel, select the channel.

2. In the lower-left corner of the **Posts** tab, select **New conversation**.

3. Type your message.

4. Select **Send** or press **Enter** or **Return**.

Does anyone know what time tomorrow's team meeting starts?

The original message of a simple conversation

To create a channel conversation with a subject

1. In the Teams panel, select the channel.

2. On the **Posts** tab, select **New conversation**.

3. At the left end of the menu bar below the conversation box, select the **Format** button to open the message editor.

4. In the **Add a subject** box, enter a subject for the conversation.

5. In the message body, enter your message.

> **TIP** In the message editor, you can press **Enter** to start a new paragraph.

6. If you want to restrict who can reply to your post, use the **Select a reply option** list to select **You and moderators can reply**.

7. Select **Send** or press **Ctrl+Enter** (Windows) or **Cmd+Return** (Mac).

> **TIP** If you decide against sending your message, you can discard it by selecting the **Delete** button.

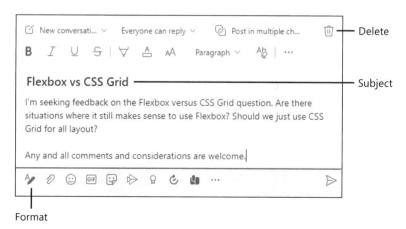

Flexbox vs CSS Grid

I'm seeking feedback on the Flexbox versus CSS Grid question. Are there situations where it still makes sense to use Flexbox? Should we just use CSS Grid for all layout?

Any and all comments and considerations are welcome.

The original message of a conversation with a subject

To create a multichannel conversation

1. In the app bar, select **Teams** to display the Teams panel.

2. Select the team name to display the team's channel list.

3. Select the channel.

4. Select the **Posts** tab.

5. Select **New conversation**.

6. Select the **Format** button to open the message editor.

7. Select **Post in multiple channels** to add a **To** line to the message.

8. Select the **Select channels** button to open the **Choose Channels** dialog.

9. Select the checkbox beside each channel you want to include in the post.

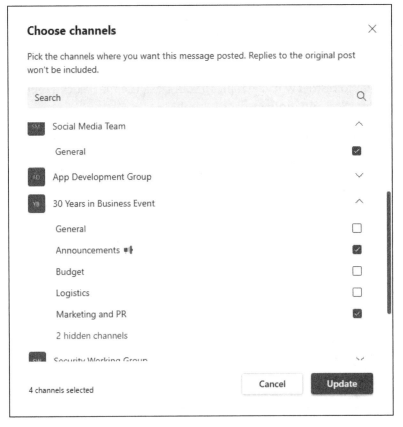

Select the checkbox beside each channel you want to include in your post.

10. Select **Update**. Teams adds the selected channels to the **To** line of the message.

11. Use the **Add a subject** text box to add a subject for the conversation.

12. Type your message in the text box. Note that in the message editor, you can press **Enter** to start a new paragraph.

13. If you want to restrict who can reply to your post, use the **Select a reply option** list to select **You and moderators can reply**.

14. Select **Send** or press **Ctrl+Enter** (Windows) or **Cmd+Return** (Mac).

 TIP If you decide against sending your message, you can discard it by selecting the **Delete** button.

4

To create a channel announcement

1. In the app bar, select **Teams** to display the Teams panel.

2. Select the team name to display the team's channel list.

3. Select the channel.

4. Select the **Posts** tab.

5. Select **New conversation**.

6. Select the **Format** button to open the message editor.

7. Use the **Select a post type** list to select **Announcement**.

8. Type a headline. You can use the **Color scheme** and **Background image** buttons to format the headline.

9. Type a subhead.

10. Type your message in the text box. Note that in the message editor, you can press **Enter** to start a new paragraph.

11. If you want to restrict who can reply to your post, use the **Select a reply option** list to select **You and moderators can reply**.

12. Select **Send** or press **Ctrl+Enter** (Windows) or **Cmd+Return** (Mac).

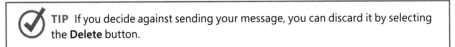

> **TIP** If you decide against sending your message, you can discard it by selecting the **Delete** button.

Select a post type

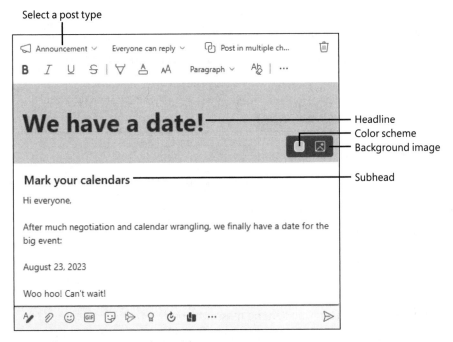

A channel announcement, ready to send

To generate an email address for a channel

1. To the right of the channel name, select **More options** (...), and then select **Get email address**.

2. In the **Get email address** dialog, select **Copy** to place a copy of the address on the Clipboard.

3. To control who can use the address, select **advanced settings**, and then select one of the following options:

   - Anyone can send emails to this address

   - Only members of this team

   - Only email sent from these domains

4. If you select the **Only email sent from these domains** option, specify the valid domains in the text box that follows the option, separating each with a comma. When you're done, select **Save**.

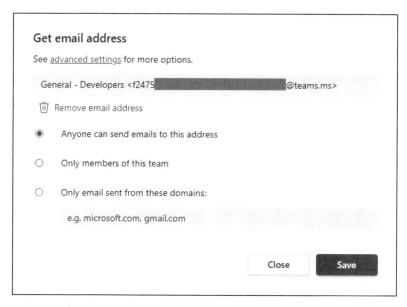

You can configure a channel email address to specify who can send messages to the address.

To share an Outlook email to a channel

1. In Outlook, select the email message you want to share.

2. In the upper-right corner of the Reading pane, select the other actions button (**…**), **Teams**, and then **Share to Teams**. You might find this command elsewhere in the Outlook ribbon depending on your version of Outlook.

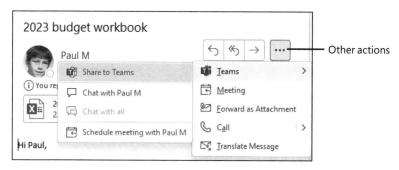

Sharing an Outlook email as a channel message

3. Use the **Share to** text box to begin typing the name of the channel to which you want to share the email, and then select the channel name when it appears in the search results.

4. In the **Type a message** text area, enter an introductory or explanatory message.

5. If you don't want to share any files that were attached to the email, clear the **Include attachments** checkbox.

6. Select **Share** to send the message to the specified channel.

7. Select **Close**.

To reply to a channel conversation

1. At the bottom of the conversation thread, select **Reply**.

2. Type your message in the text box.

3. Select **Send** or press **Enter** or **Return**.

Enhance channel messages

Channel messages are a great way to address a comment or query to every member of a channel. Many of those conversations will be quick exchanges of information, so the messages will be simple: unformatted text with no special features. However, in an active channel with many conversations, your message might get lost in a busy Posts tab if it doesn't stand out from the rest of the conversations. You can help make it harder for people to miss or ignore your message if you apply a judicious amount of text formatting and special features such as emojis and stickers.

> **SEE ALSO** One message enhancement that I don't cover in this chapter is attaching a file to a message. To learn how to do that, see "Manage files and folders" in Chapter 6, "Work with files."

> **IMPORTANT** Teams offers a rich palette of message enhancements. However, just as a plain message might get missed because it doesn't stand out, an overly formatted message festooned with emojis and animated GIFs might get skipped because it stands out *too* much. Balance is the key here: Try to use enough enhancements to get your post noticed and strengthen your message, but avoid extraneous adornments that add nothing to your message.

Format channel message text

Whether you're composing an original channel message or replying to an existing message, you start out with a basic text box. Although this text box presents no formatting controls, you can still format selected message text as follows:

- Press **Ctrl+B** (Windows) or **Cmd+B** (Mac) to make the selected text bold.

- Press **Ctrl+I** (Windows) or **Cmd+I** (Mac) to make the selected text italic.

- Press **Ctrl+U** (Windows) or **Cmd+U** (Mac) to make the selected text underlined.

However, if you want to format your message text, it's usually faster and easier to display the message editor, which includes a toolbar with various formatting controls. You display the message editor by selecting the Format button.

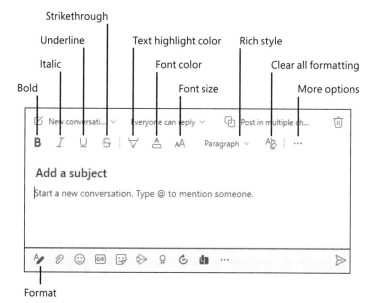

The text formatting options in the channel message editor

The message editor toolbar offers the following controls:

- **Bold**   Toggles bold on and off for the selected text.

- **Italic**   Toggles italic on and off for the selected text.

- **Underline**   Toggles underlining on and off for the selected text.

- **Strikethrough**   Toggles strikethrough on and off for the selected text.

- **Text highlight color**   Displays a palette so you can select a color for the background of the selected text.

- **Font color**   Displays a palette so you can select a color for the selected text.

- **Font size**   Displays a list so you can choose the size of the selected text: **Large**, **Medium**, or **Small**.

- **Rich style**   Displays a list so you can apply a style to the selected text: **Heading 1**, **Heading 2**, **Heading 3**, **Paragraph** (that is, regular text), or **Monospaced**.

- **Clear all formatting**   Removes all formatting applied to the selected text.

- **More options**   Displays a menu of options for enhancing text, most of which I cover in the next section, "Structure channel message content." If your screen uses a wide resolution, you might not see the **More options** button; instead, all the buttons will appear on the message editor toolbar.

> ✓ **TIP** Although you usually apply the formatting options to selected text, if you want to apply some formatting to the next text you type, position the insertion point where you want to start typing and then select the formatting you want to use.

To format channel message text

1. Below an unposted channel message, select the **Format** button to display the message editor and its toolbar.

2. Select the text you want to format or position the insertion point where you want to apply the formatting to the text you're about to type.

3. Use the controls on the message editor toolbar to apply the formatting.

4. If you're typing formatted text and you want the next text you type to have no formatting, select the **Clear all formatting** button on the toolbar.

Structure channel message content

It's unlikely that you'll want to spend a lot of time working on the structure of a channel message, but there will be times when modifying the structure can help you get your message across. For example, if your message includes a list of items, you'll likely want to present those items as a bulleted list. Similarly, if you're going through a series of steps in your message, those steps will be much easier to follow if you structure them as a numbered list.

4

Here's a quick look at the types of structural changes you can make to the content of the channel message:

- **Indent text**   Increasing the indent shifts the left edge of the current paragraph to the right; similarly, decreasing the indent shifts the left edge of the current paragraph to the left.

- **Bulleted list**   Arranges the selected text as a list of items, where each item is a paragraph from the selected text, and each item is preceded by a *bullet* (a small, black dot).

- **Numbered list**   Arranges the selected text as a numbered sequence of items, where each item is a paragraph from the selected text, and each item is preceded by a number, where the first paragraph is 1, the second paragraph is 2, and so on.

- **Quoted text**   Displays the selected paragraph indented with a light gray background and a dark gray left border. Use this structure if you want to include in your message a quotation from another person or work.

- **Link**   Converts text into a link to a web page.

- **Code snippet**   Inserts one or more lines of code, where the text is in a monospace font with a light gray background, and each line is numbered.

- **Horizontal rule**   Inserts a gray, horizontal line across the width of the message editor. Use horizontal rules to separate sections of your message.

- **Table**   Organizes text into a row-and-column format.

- **Mark a message as important**   Adds the text IMPORTANT! above the message to let others know that your message contains essential or not-to-be-missed information.

These message options are available via the message editor toolbar, which you display by selecting the **Format** button in an original message or a reply. Note that, depending on your screen resolution width, you might have to select the **More options** toolbar button (...) to see some or all of the options.

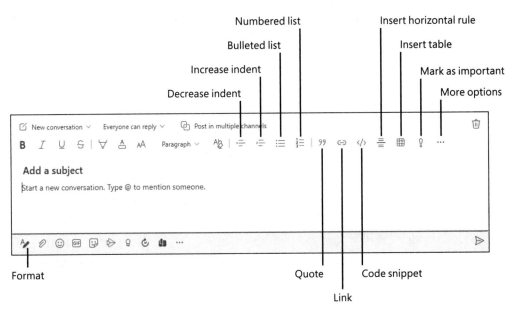

The message structure options in the channel message editor

To increase the indent of text in a channel message

1. Select the text you want to indent:

   - If you're indenting just a single paragraph, place the insertion point anywhere inside that paragraph.

   - If you're indenting two or more paragraphs, select at least one character in each paragraph.

2. On the message editor toolbar, select **Increase indent**.

3. Repeat Step 2 until the text is indented as much as you want.

To decrease the indent of text in a channel message

1. Select the text for which you want to decrease the indent:

   - If you're working with just a single paragraph, place the insertion point anywhere inside that paragraph.

   - If you're working with two or more paragraphs, select at least one character in each paragraph.

2. On the message editor toolbar, select **Decrease indent**.

3. Repeat Step 2 until the text indentation is decreased as much as you want.

To add a bulleted list to a channel message

1. Position the insertion point where you want the bulleted list to appear. If you want to convert existing text to a bulleted list, select that text.

2. On the message editor toolbar, select **Bulleted list**. If you converted existing text to a bulleted list and you want to add more items, position the insertion point at the end of the last item and skip to Step 4.

3. Type your item text.

4. Press **Enter** or **Return**. Teams adds a new item to the bulleted list.

5. Repeat Steps 3 and 4 until your bulleted list is complete.

6. In the final (empty) item, press **Enter** or **Return** a second time to complete the bulleted list.

To add a numbered list to a channel message

1. Position the insertion point where you want the numbered list to appear. If you want to convert existing text to a numbered list, select that text.

2. On the message editor toolbar, select **Numbered list**. If you converted existing text to a numbered list and you want to add more items, position the insertion point at the end of the last item and skip to Step 4.

3. Enter the list item text, and then press **Enter** or **Return**. Teams adds a new item to the numbered list.

4. Repeat Step 3 until your numbered list is complete.

5. In the final (empty) item, press **Enter** or **Return** a second time to complete the numbered list.

To add quoted text to a channel message

1. Position the insertion point where you want the quotation to appear. If you want to convert existing text to a quotation, select that text.

2. On the message editor toolbar, select **Quote**. If you converted existing text to a quotation, you're done.

3. Type or paste your quotation text.

To add a link to a channel message

1. Select the text that you want to convert to a link.

2. On the message editor toolbar, select **Link**.

3. In the **Insert Link** dialog, edit the link text in the **Text to display** box, if necessary.

4. Type or paste the link address in the **Address** text box.

5. Select **Insert**.

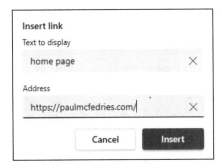

Use the Insert Link dialog to add a link to a channel message.

To add a code snippet to a channel message

1. Position the insertion point where you want the code snippet to appear in your channel message.

2. On the message editor toolbar, select **Code snippet** to display the code snippet dialog.

3. Type a title for the code.

4. From the list in the upper-right corner, select the type of code you're adding.

5. Enter your code in the large text box.

6. Select **Insert**.

CSS for a drop cap ☐ Wrap text Text ⌄

```
 1 ▾ * {
 2       margin: 0;
 3       padding: 0;
 4       box-sizing: border-box;
 5       font-size: 100%;
 6   }
 7 ▾ body {
 8       width: 550px;
 9       color: #444;
10       font-family: Georgia, serif;
11       font-size: 1.1em;
12       line-height: 1.4;
13   }
14 ▾ div {
15       margin: 1em;
16       padding: 1em;
17   }
18 ▾ .first-paragraph::first-letter {
19       float: left;
20       padding-top: .1em;
21       padding-right: .1em;
22       color: darkred;
23       font-size: 5em;
24       line-height: .6em;
25   }
```

Cancel   Insert

Use this dialog to add a code snippet to a channel message.

To add a horizontal rule to a channel message

1. Position the insertion point in the paragraph above which you want the horizontal rule to appear in your channel message.

2. On the message editor toolbar, select **Insert horizontal rule**.

To insert a table into a channel message

1. Position the insertion point where you want the table to appear in your channel message.

2. On the message editor toolbar, select **Insert table**.

3. On the menu that appears, point to the square that indicates the number of columns and rows you want in your table, and then select the square to insert the table.

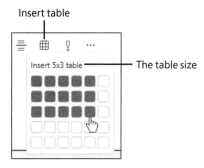

Select Insert table and then select
the size of the table you want.

To mark a message as important

- On the message editor toolbar, select **Mark as important**.

Work with @mentions

Channel conversations are a useful and efficient way to exchange information on a particular topic. However, for all but the smallest channels, the Posts tab can get very busy with multiple conversations going on at the same time. If you're posting a message that must be seen by someone, how can you ensure that person will actually see (much less read) your message?

There are no guarantees, but one method that can help is to @mention that person in your message. In a channel message, when you type @ and then start typing a person's name, Teams displays a Suggestions list that includes the members that match your typing. When you see the person you want, click the name to complete the @mention. Now, when you post your message, the member who is the subject of the @mention will receive a Teams notification. The member only has to select that notification to display the message.

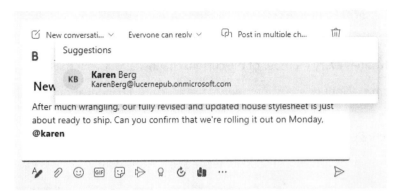

Type @, followed by the start of the person's name, and then click the name you want in the Suggestions list.

When someone includes an @mention for you in a message, two things happen:

- You receive a Teams notification.

- You see a white-on-red @ icon next to the message with your @mention.

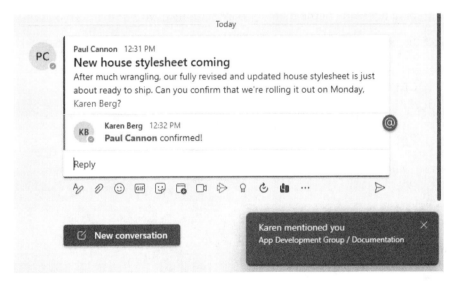

When someone @mentions you, you receive a Teams notification, and an @ icon appears next to the message.

 TIP To see a list of all your @mentions, type /mentions in the Teams **Search** box and then press **Enter** or **Return**.

95

Although the majority of @mentions are aimed at people, there are also four other types of @mention you can use:

- **@channel**   Notifies every member of the current channel about your message.
- **@***channel_name***   Notifies every member of the specified channel about your message.
- **@team**   Notifies every member of the current team about your message.
- **@***team_name***   Notifies every member of the specified team about your message.

> ⚠️ **IMPORTANT** Channel and team @mentions are powerful tools that should be used only when truly necessary. This is particularly true of team @mentions, which are the Teams equivalent of organization-wide Reply All email messages.

To add an @mention to a channel message

1. Type @.
2. Start typing the name of the person, channel, or team you want to @mention.
3. Select the person, channel, or team when it appears in the Suggestions list.

Add a reaction to an existing channel message

Rather than replying to a channel message, you can send one of the following reactions:

- Like
- Heart (love)
- Laugh
- Surprised
- Sad
- Angry

The reaction appears in the upper-right corner of the channel message, followed by a number that indicates how many people have sent the same reaction.

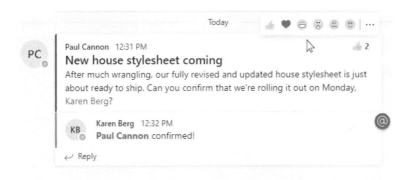

Point to a channel message to see the available reactions.

To add a reaction to a channel message

■ Point to the channel message to display the reaction toolbar, and then select the button that represents the reaction you want to send.

Add special features to channel messages

Teams also enables you to augment your channel messages with a few special features:

■ Emojis

■ Animated GIFs (via the Giphy service)

■ Stickers

■ Memes

As with text formatting, exercise some care with these special features since including too many of them can make your message less likely to be read or taken seriously.

Teams offers several special features that you can add to a channel message.

To add an emoji to a channel message

1. Position the insertion point where you want the emoji to appear.

2. Select the **Emoji** button.

3. Select the emoji you want to add.

To add an animated GIF to a channel message

1. Position the insertion point where you want the animated GIF to appear.

2. Select the **Giphy** button.

3. Select the animated GIF you want to add.

To add a sticker to a channel message

1. Position the insertion point where you want the sticker to appear.

2. Select the **Sticker** button.

3. Select a category.

4. Select the sticker you want to add.

Teams offers several categories of stickers.

To add a meme to a channel message

1. Position the insertion point where you want the meme to appear.

2. Select the **Sticker** button.

3. Select the **Meme** category.

4. Select the meme image you want to use.

 TIP To upload your own meme image, select **Upload** (+), select the image in the Open dialog that appears, and then select **Open**.

5. Type a top caption.

6. Type a bottom caption.

7. Select **Done**.

Select a meme image, and then add your own captions.

Manage channel messages

To help keep your channel conversations relevant and orderly, Teams offers quite a few message management commands. Here are a half dozen of the most useful commands:

- **Edit**   Select this command to modify one of your channel messages. Use this command when you need to correct an error, add new text, or delete existing text.

- **Pin**   Select this command to add a channel message to the Pinned Posts section of the channel's Info panel.

- **Save this message**   Select this command to save a copy of a channel message in your Teams profile's Saved panel.

- **Share to Outlook**   Select this command to copy a channel message to an Outlook email message.

- **Turn on notifications**   Select this command to receive a notification every time someone responds to a channel message that someone else posted.

- **Delete**   Select this command to remove one of your messages from a channel conversation.

To edit a channel message

1. Point to the channel message you want to edit.

2. Select **More options** (...), and then select **Edit** to open the channel message for editing.

3. Make your changes to the channel message, and then select **Done** (the check mark button).

To pin a channel message

1. Point to the channel message you want to pin.

2. Select **More options** (...), and then select **Pin**.

> **IMPORTANT** To see a channel's pinned posts, select the **Show channel info** button (the i-in-a-circle in the upper-right corner of the channel).

To save a channel message

1. Point to the channel message you want to save.

2. Select **More options (…)**, and then select **Save this message**.

> ⚠️ **IMPORTANT** To access your saved channel messages, select your Teams avatar and then select **Saved**. Alternatively, type /saved in the Teams **Search** box and then press **Enter** or **Return**.

4

To share a channel message via Outlook

1. Point to the channel message you want to share.

2. Select **More options (…)**, and then select **Share to Outlook**. Teams creates a new Outlook email message.

3. Address the email message.

4. Edit the subject line if needed. Note that Teams uses the channel conversation subject as the email subject line.

5. Precede the channel message with explanatory text, if needed.

6. Select **Send**.

To turn on notifications for a channel conversation

1. Point to the channel message for which you want to receive notifications.

2. Select **More options (…)**, and then select **Turn on notifications**.

To delete a channel message

1. Point to the channel message you want to delete.

2. Select **More options (…)**, and then select **Delete**.

Key points

- Although simple channel messages are fine for brief exchanges, to get the most out of channel messages, be sure to select the Format button to access all the message tools.

- When posting an original channel message, it's best to use a subject so that other channel members know what your post is about.

- Remember that the General channel is accessible to all team members, so only post to that channel if your message is suitable for or relevant to everyone on the team.

- Teams offers a wide variety of features to enhance and augment channel messages, but don't go overboard; only use a feature if it adds value to your message.

- Using an @mention for a person is a useful tool for helping ensure your message is read, but you should use channel and team @mentions only rarely.

Extend Teams with apps and services

When you start up a new Windows or Mac computer, it comes with a default collection of programs that enable you to perform most basic computing tasks. However, it's a rare user whose computing experience is satisfied by just the operating system's default software. Most people extend the operating system by installing programs that make their computers more productive, more efficient, more useful, and more fun.

The business and enterprise versions of Microsoft Teams are the same way: They come with a default collection of apps that enable you to perform all the basic Teams tasks, such as chatting, setting up and managing teams and channels, managing your schedule, making phone calls, and working with files. But Teams is a platform, which means you can extend it well beyond these basic use cases by installing Microsoft and third-party apps and services.

In this chapter, you learn about the different types of apps that you can use with Teams, and you learn how to extend Teams with personal apps, tabs, messaging extensions, connectors, and bots.

In this chapter
- Understand and manage apps
- Extend Teams with personal apps
- Extend Teams with tabs
- Extend Teams with messaging extensions
- Extend Teams with connectors
- Extend Teams with bots

Understand and manage apps

One of the secrets to productivity is to minimize *task-switching*, where you exchange one set of digital tools for another when you switch to a new task. The problem with task-switching is that it comes with a high cost that's measured in both time and cognitive load as you orient yourself to each new environment and its different interface and features.

So, if you're wondering why you'd ever want to extend Teams with apps, the short answer is that you can greatly reduce task-switching. Here are some example scenarios:

- If you're working on a big personal project as part of a team and you have a large number of tasks to keep track of, you can install the Tasks by Planner and To Do app within Teams rather than relying on an external to-do list app.

- If you and your team are collaborating on a OneNote notebook, you can add that notebook as a channel tab for easy team access.

- If you regularly use Microsoft Forms to solicit feedback from your team, you can extend channel conversations with the Forms app so that you can create forms within Teams itself.

- If you and your team are interested in posts from a particular blog, you can add the RSS connector to a channel, which means every new entry from the blog gets posted to the channel.

- If your team uses Power Automate flows to automate repetitive tasks, you can invoke Power Automate from within a channel message to list the available flows and run a particular flow.

In each of these scenarios, you bring the task or tasks within the Teams platform, so you eliminate at least some task-switching costs, and you boost overall team productivity.

The key to getting a solid grip on Teams app integration is to understand that the word *app* in Teams really refers to six different ways of integrating apps and services within the platform:

- **Personal apps**   These are apps that you use personally as part of your Teams experience. Personal apps are integrated into the Teams app bar.

- **Tabs**   These are apps that appear as tabs at the top of a channel or chat window. For example, by default, all new channels created from scratch come with tabs for the Files and Wiki apps.

- **Messaging extensions** These are apps that appear in the row of icons below the compose window for a channel or chat message. These extensions enable you to post app content—such as a form created with the Microsoft Forms app—to a channel or chat conversation.

- **Meeting extensions** These are apps that are available during a meeting.

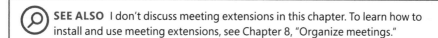 **SEE ALSO** I don't discuss meeting extensions in this chapter. To learn how to install and use meeting extensions, see Chapter 8, "Organize meetings."

5

- **Connectors** These apps enable a channel to connect to content and data provided by a particular service. A popular example is posting the entries of an RSS feed via the RSS connector.

- **Bots** These apps enable you to interact with other apps and services using commands supported by the bot.

It's important to understand that an app might support multiple integration types. For example, when you install an app, it might add a tab to a channel, offer a connector to app data, and include a bot for interacting with the service.

 SEE ALSO You can gain some control over Teams apps by setting their permissions. To learn how to do this, see "Customize app permissions" in Chapter 12, "Customize teams."

Teams supports three types of apps:

- **Microsoft apps** Apps developed by Microsoft.

- **Third-party apps** Apps developed by companies other than Microsoft.

- **Custom apps** Apps developed by (or for) your organization. Most custom apps are developed using a Microsoft Power Platform low-code development tool such as Power Apps.

TIP The Teams app store offers an app called Power Apps that enables you to build custom apps right within the Teams environment. Building custom Teams apps is beyond the scope of this book. See *https://docs.microsoft.com/en-us/powerapps/teams/overview* to get started.

Teams gives you various ways to install and manage apps, but the most common and easiest method is the Teams app store, which you display by selecting Apps in the app bar. In the Store panel that appears, you can search for the app you want, or you can select a link in the Featured, Categories, or Industries sections.

> **SEE ALSO** By default, Teams allows every team member (but not team guests) to install any Microsoft, third-party, or custom app. If you're a Teams administrator, you can allow and/or block specific apps. To learn how to do this, see "Manage Teams via policies" in Chapter 13, "Administer Teams."

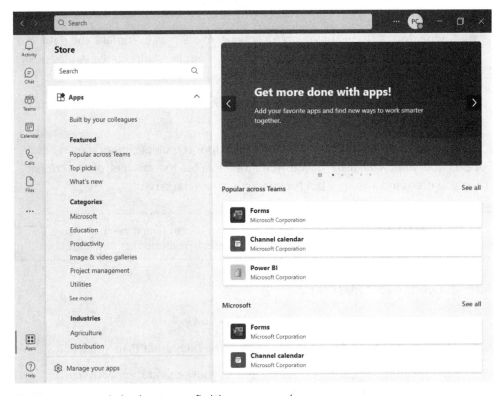

The Teams app store is the place to go to find the app you need.

> **TIP** If your organization has custom Teams apps, you can see them in the app store by selecting the **Built by your colleagues** link in the Store panel.

> **SEE ALSO** You can enhance your Teams privacy by setting permissions on what each app is allowed to do and what resources each app can access. See "Customize app permissions" in Chapter 12, "Customize Teams."

To open the app store

- Select **Apps** in the Teams app bar.

- Select **More added apps** in the Teams app bar, and then select **More apps**.

- In the Teams panel, select **More options** to the right of a team name, select **Manage team**, select the **Apps** tab, and then select **More apps**.

To view a team's apps

1. Select **Teams** in the app bar to open the Teams panel.

2. Select **More options** to the right of the team name.

3. Select **Manage team**.

4. Select the **Apps** tab.

To uninstall a team app

1. Select **Teams** in the app bar to open the Teams panel.

2. Select **More options** to the right of the team name.

3. Select **Manage team**.

4. Select the **Apps** tab.

5. Select the **Uninstall** (trash can) icon to the right of the app.

6. When Teams asks you to confirm, select **Uninstall**.

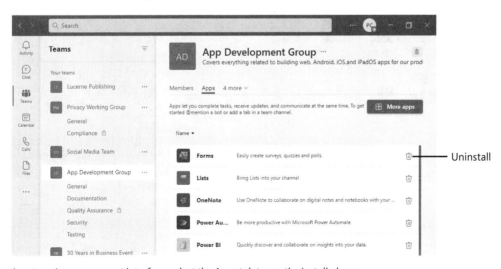

In a team's management interface, select the Apps tab to see the installed apps.

Extend Teams with personal apps

Your Teams subscription comes with several preinstalled personal apps, including OneNote, Wiki (to create and edit wiki content); Tasks by Planner and To Do (to manage tasks); Shifts (to create team schedules); Stream (to stream video content); and Approvals (to create and route approvals). To access these and all your personal apps, select the **More added apps** icon in the app bar.

 TIP You can also open the list of personal apps by pressing **Ctrl+`** (backtick) or **Cmd+`** (backtick).

More added apps

Select the More added apps button to see your installed personal apps.

Install personal apps

Unfortunately, the Teams app store doesn't have a separate section or category just for personal apps, nor does it have any way to search for personal apps. The only way to tell whether an app is a personal app is to open its information window (by selecting the app in the app store) and then look for a section named **Personal app**.

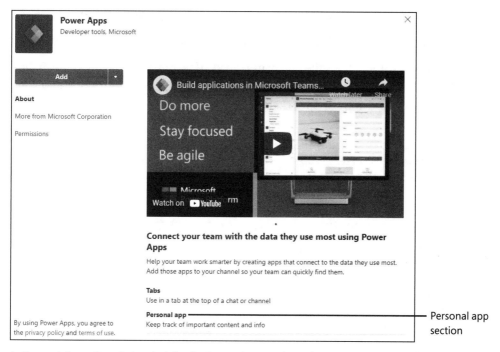

Personal app section

In the app information window, look for the Personal app section to know you're installing a personal app.

To install a personal app

1. Display the Teams app store.

2. Select the app you want to install.

3. Select **Add**. Teams installs the app.

To uninstall a personal app

1. If the app icon is not currently displayed on the app bar, select **More added apps**.

2. Right-click the app you want to uninstall.

3. Select **Uninstall**. Teams asks you to confirm.

4. Select **Uninstall**.

Customize the app bar

When you open an installed personal app, Teams adds the app's icon to the app bar temporarily, which means that the icon disappears from the app bar as soon as you switch to another Teams app. While the app's icon is on the app bar, you have several options for working with the app and its icon:

- **Pin the app icon**   Gives the app's icon a permanent place on the app bar.

- **Move the app icon**   Positions the app icon up or down within the app bar.

- **Pop out the app**   Runs the app in its own window rather than embedded in the Teams window. Note that, with the exception of Chat, this feature is not available for the standard app bar apps (Activity, Teams, Calendar, Calls, and Files).

> ⚠ IMPORTANT If you move one or more app bar icons, this affects the keyboard shortcuts that you use to select app bar items. For example, by default, pressing **Ctrl+1** or **Cmd+1** selects the **Activity** icon. However, these shortcuts actually select the *first* app bar item. So, for example, if you pin the OneNote app and then move it to the top of the app bar, pressing **Ctrl+1** or **Cmd+1** now selects OneNote.

To pin an app icon

1. If the app icon is not currently displayed on the app bar, select **More added apps**.

2. Right-click the app you want to pin.

3. Select **Pin**. The app icon now remains on the app bar even when you switch to a different Teams app.

To unpin an app icon

1. On the app bar, right-click the app's pinned icon.

2. Select **Unpin**. Teams now removes the app icon from the app bar when you switch to a different Teams app.

To move an app icon

1. Pin the app icon if you haven't done so already.

2. Click and drag the app icon vertically within the app bar until the icon is in the position you want.

3. Release the icon to move the app.

To pop out an app

1. If the app icon is not currently displayed on the app bar, select **More added apps**.

2. Right-click the app you want to pop out.

3. Select **Pop out app**. If you're working with Chat, select **Pop out new chat**, instead. Teams opens the app in its own window.

Extend Teams with tabs

Since so much of your work with Teams takes place in one channel or another, an easy way to avoid the costs of task-switching is to bring as much "external" work as possible into a channel where members can access the work without having to switch to another app. The way you give channel members quick and easy access to such work is by adding a new tab for the work.

Add a channel tab

You can add three types of channel tabs:

-   **App** This type of tab enables channel members to work with an app to create new content or modify existing content. A popular example is the Channel Calendar app, which enables channel members to view and add events to a common calendar.

-   **File** This type of tab enables channel members to collaborate on a single file, such as a Word, Excel, PowerPoint, or PDF file.

 IMPORTANT Before you can add a file as a tab, the file must be uploaded to the channel.

 SEE ALSO To learn how to upload files to a channel, see "Create files and folders" in Chapter 6, "Work with files."

- **Info** This type of tab enables channel members to view content, such as a web page or a YouTube video.

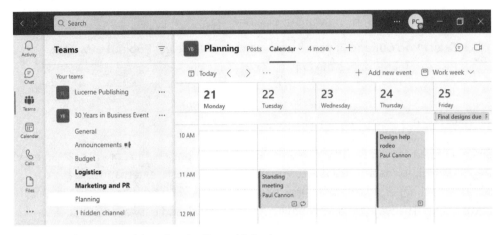

A channel with a custom tab based on the Channel Calendar app

To add a channel tab from the app store

1. Display the app store.

2. Select the app you want to install.

3. Select **Add to a team**. If you only see the **Add** button, drop down the **Add** list and select **Add to a team**. Teams prompts you for the team and channel name.

> 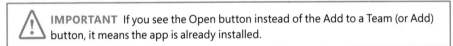 **IMPORTANT** If you see the Open button instead of the Add to a Team (or Add) button, it means the app is already installed.

4. Enter the team name and then, from the list that appears, select the channel to which you want to add the new tab.

5. Select **Set up a tab**. Teams prompts you for a tab name.

6. Enter a short tab name.

7. Select **Add**. Teams adds the new tab to the channel.

To add a channel tab from the channel

1. In the channel, select **Add a tab (+)**.

2. In the **Add a Tab** window, select the app you want to add.

3. Install the app:

- If the app requires a tab name and other information, enter the required data (the specifics of which vary, depending on the app) and then select **Save**.

- Otherwise, select **Add**.

To add a Microsoft 365 document as a tab

1. In the channel to which you want to add the Microsoft 365 document, select **Add a tab** (+).

2. In the **Add a tab** window, select the app you want to add: **Word**, **Excel**, or **PowerPoint**.

3. In the app-specific dialog:

   a. Enter the tab name.

   b. Select the file you want to appear in the tab.

   c. Select **Save**.

You can augment a channel with a custom tab based on a Microsoft 365 document.

To add a PDF file as a tab

1. In the channel, select **Add a tab** (+).

2. In the **Add a tab** window, select the **PDF** app.

3. In the **PDF** dialog:

   a. Enter the tab name.

   b. Select the PDF file you want to appear in the tab.

   c. Select **Save**.

To add a website as a tab

1. In the channel, select **Add a tab** (+).

2. In the **Add a tab** window, select the **Website** app.

3. In the **Website** dialog:

   a. Enter the tab name.

   b. Enter or paste the website URL.

   c. Select **Save**.

To add a YouTube video as a tab

1. In the channel, select **Add a tab** (+).

2. In the **Add a tab** window, select the **YouTube** app.

3. Enter or paste the YouTube video URL and then press **Enter** or **Return**.

4. Select **Save**.

> ✓ **TIP** The YouTube app doesn't give you a way to specify the tab name while adding the tab, which is too bad since YouTube video tab names are often quite long. However, you can edit the name after you add the tab, as described in the following section.

Work with a custom tab

Once you have an app or a file added to a channel as a custom tab, you display the tab by navigating to the channel and then selecting the tab. Teams then gives you several ways to work with your custom tab, including the following:

- Expanding the tab so that it takes up the entire Teams window (except for the app bar)

- Refreshing the tab so that it contains the most recent content

- Sharing a link to the tab so that another person can navigate directly to the tab

- Renaming the tab

- Customizing the tab's settings (if any)

- Removing the tab

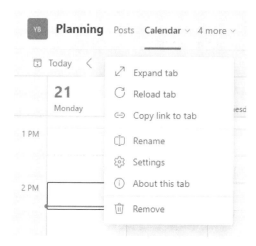

Select a custom tab's dropdown arrow to see a list of actions you can perform on the tab.

To expand a tab

1. Select the tab.

2. Select the **Tab Options** arrow to the right of the tab name, and then select **Expand tab**.

To refresh a tab

1. Select the tab.

2. Select the **Tab Options** arrow to the right of the tab name, and then select **Reload tab**.

To share a link to a tab

1. Select the tab.

2. Select the **Tab Options** arrow to the right of the tab name, and then select **Copy link to tab**. Teams copies the tab link to the Clipboard.

3. Paste the link into the message you want to use to share the link.

4. Address and send the message.

To rename a tab

1. Select the tab.

2. Select the **Tab Options** arrow to the right of the tab name, and then select **Rename**.

3. Enter a new name for the tab, and then select **Save**.

To adjust a tab's settings

1. Select the tab.

2. Select the **Tab Options** arrow to the right of the tab name, and then select **Settings**.

3. Adjust the tab settings, and then select **Save**.

To remove a tab

1. Select the tab.

2. Select the **Tab Options** arrow to the right of the tab name, and then select **Remove**.

3. When Teams asks you to confirm, select **Remove**.

Extend Teams with messaging extensions

A *messaging extension* is a Teams app type that enables you to post app content directly into a channel or chat conversation. For example, if a debate ensues in a channel conversation, you might want to take a quick poll of the channel members to see where everyone stands. With the Microsoft Forms messaging extension, you can quickly create a simple poll and post it to the channel.

Install messaging extensions

The Teams app store doesn't have a separate section or category for messaging extensions, nor does it have any way to search for messaging extensions. The only way to know whether an app is a messaging extension is to select the app in the app store. In the app's information window, look for a section named **Messages**.

> ⚠️ **IMPORTANT** It's a rare app that only installs a messaging extension. Most apps that include a messaging extension component will also install a personal app, a channel tab, a connector, a bot, or some combination of all these app types.

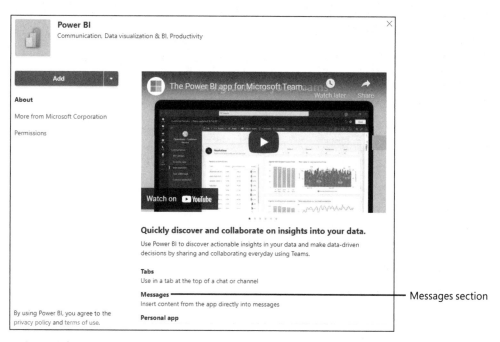

In the app information window, look for the Messages section to know you're installing a messaging extension.

To install a messaging extension

1. Display the app store.

2. Select the app you want to install as a messaging extension.

3. Select **Add**. Teams installs the messaging extension.

To uninstall a messaging extension

1. Start a new conversation or a reply to an existing conversation to display the messaging extensions.

2. In the row of icons under the text box, select **Messaging extensions** (...).

3. Right-click the messaging extension icon you want to uninstall.

4. Select **Uninstall**. Teams asks you to confirm.

5. Select **Uninstall**.

Work with messaging extensions

Once you have a messaging extension added, you use it by starting a new conversation or reply, and then selecting the messaging extension from the row of icons beneath the text box. If you find this row of icons becoming unwieldy, you can temporarily hide an icon by unpinning it. The messaging extension is still available, but it now takes an extra click to access it. When you're ready to see the messaging extension below the message text box once again, you can pin the icon.

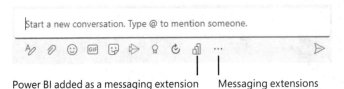

Power BI added as a messaging extension   Messaging extensions

Messaging extensions appear as icons below the message text box.

To send content from a messaging extension to a channel or chat conversation

1. Start a new conversation or a reply to an existing conversation.

2. If the message extension is pinned, select its icon below the message box; otherwise, select **Messaging extensions (...)** and then select the icon.

3. In the app interface that appears, create the content you want to send.

4. Select **Preview**.

5. Select **Send**. The messaging extension posts the content to the channel or chat conversation.

To pin a messaging extension

1. Start a new conversation or a reply to an existing conversation to display the messaging extensions.

2. Select **Messaging extensions (...)**.

3. Right-click the messaging extension icon you want to pin.

4. Select **Pin**. The messaging extension icon now appears below the message text box.

To unpin a messaging extension

1. Start a new conversation or a reply to an existing conversation to display the messaging extensions.

2. Right-click the messaging extension you want to unpin.

3. Select **Unpin**. Teams hides the messaging extension icon.

5

Extend Teams with connectors

A *connector* is an app feature that enables a channel to connect to content provided by an external service. New content appears as a notification within the channel's Posts tab in card format. A popular example of a connector is the RSS app, which posts new RSS feed items to a channel on a specified schedule.

 TIP You can tell connector notifications from channel member posts by noting that member avatars are circles while connector avatars are hexagons.

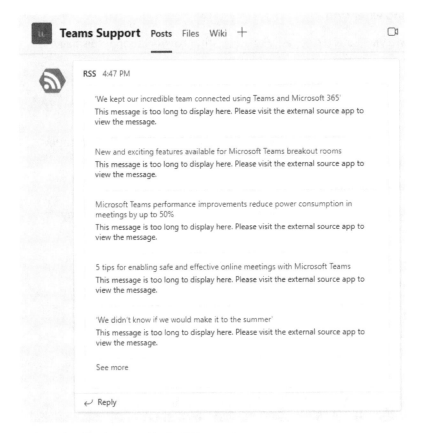

A channel notification posted by the RSS connector

Install a connector

Teams gives you two options for installing connectors:

- **Via a channel** This is the easiest route because each channel offers a Connectors command that displays a dialog that lists all the available connectors.

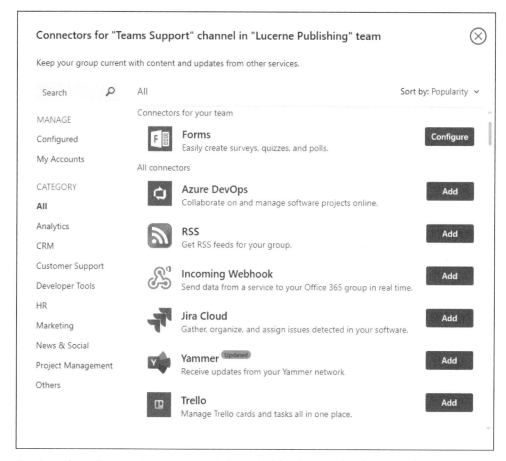

Running a channel's Connectors command displays this dialog that contains all the available connectors.

- **Via the app store** This is the more involved method because the app store doesn't have a separate section or category for connectors, nor does it have any way to search for connectors. The only way to know whether an app is a connector is to select the app in the app store. In the app's information window, look for a section named **Notifications**.

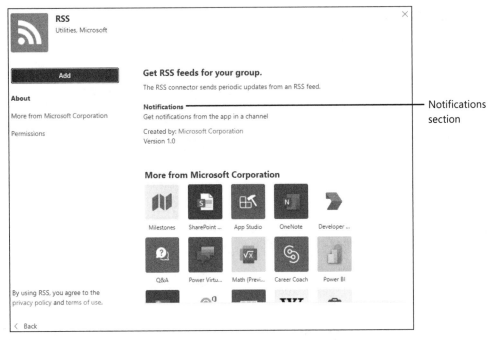

Notifications section

In the app information window, look for the Notifications section to know you're installing a connector.

To install a connector from a channel

1. In the app bar, select **Teams** to open the Teams panel.

2. Select the team to display its channels.

3. Select **More options** (...) to the right of the channel in which you want to install the connector.

4. Select **Connectors** to display a dialog that lists all the available connectors.

5. Locate the connector and then select its **Add** button. Teams displays the app store information window for the app.

6. Select **Add**.

To install a connector from the app store

1. Display the app store.

2. Select the app that contains the connector you want to install.

3. Select **Add to a team**. If you only see the Add button, drop down the **Add** list and select **Add to a team**. Teams prompts you for the team and channel name.

4. Enter the team name, and then, from the list that appears, select the channel to which you want to add the new tab.

5. Select **Set up**. Teams install the app and adds the connector to the specified channel.

Configure a connector

Installing a connector is only the first step because all you've done is made the connector available to a particular channel. The next step is to configure the connector. For example, if you added the RSS connector to a channel, you now need to configure the connector with a name, the URL of an RSS feed, and an update frequency.

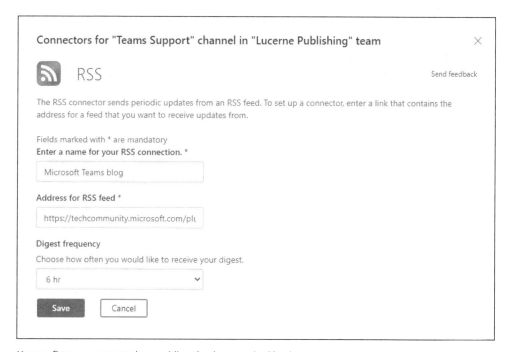

You configure a connector by providing the data required by the connector.

To configure a connector

1. In the app bar, select **Teams** to open the Teams panel.

2. Select the team to display its channels.

3. Select **More options** (...) to the right of the channel in which you want to install the connector.

4. Select **Connectors** to display a dialog that lists all the available connectors.

5. In the **Connectors for your team** section, select the **Configure** button next to the connector you want to set up.

6. Fill in the information required by the connector. (The fields you see will vary depending on the connector.)

7. Select **Save**.

Manage connectors

After you configure a connector, it now appears in the **Configured** section of the **Connectors** dialog. You manage your connectors from the **Configured** section, and Teams enables you to perform the following connector management tasks:

- **Add another configuration** Although for most connectors, you only run through the configuration process once, many connectors support multiple configurations. For the RSS connector, for example, you can configure multiple RSS feeds for a single channel.

- **Modify a configuration** You can edit an existing configuration to change the underlying data required by the connector.

- **Remove a configuration** If you no longer need or use a connector configuration, you can remove it so that you no longer see its notifications in your channel.

Your configured connectors appear in the Configured section of the Connectors dialog.

To add another configuration to a connector

1. In the app bar, select **Teams** to open the Teams panel.

2. Select the team to display its channels.

3. Select **More options** (...) to the right of the channel in which you want to install the connector.

4. Select **Connectors** to display a dialog that lists all the available connectors.

5. Select the **Configured** category.

6. Select the **Configure** button next to the connector you want to configure.

7. Fill in the information required by the connector.

8. Select **Save**.

To modify a connector configuration

1. In the app bar, select **Teams** to open the **Teams** panel.

2. Select the team to display its channels.

3. Select **More options** (...) to the right of the channel in which you want to install the connector.

4. Select **Connectors** to display a dialog that lists all the available connectors.

5. Select the **Configured** category.

6. For the connector you want to work with, select the *x* **configured** link, where *x* is the number of configurations already defined for the connector.

7. Select the **Manage** button next to the configuration you want to work with.

8. Edit the connector information as needed.

9. Select **Save**.

To remove a connector configuration

1. In the app bar, select **Teams** to open the **Teams** panel.

2. Select the team to display its channels.

3. Select **More options** (...) to the right of the channel in which you want to install the connector.

5

4. Select **Connectors** to display a dialog that lists all the available connectors.

5. Select the **Configured** category.

6. For the connector you want to work with, select the *x* **configured** link, where *x* is the number of configurations already defined for the connector.

7. Select the **Manage** button next to the configuration you want to remove.

8. Select **Remove**. The **Remove Configuration** dialog appears.

9. Select the checkbox beside each reason that applies for wanting to remove the configuration and add any extra comments you want to share.

10. Select **Remove**.

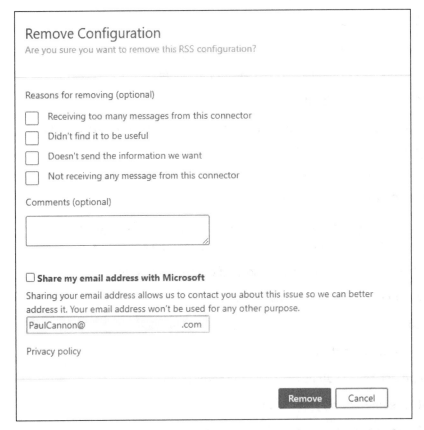

You can optionally let Microsoft know the reasons why you're removing this configuration.

Extend Teams with bots

A *bot* is an app feature that enables you to interact with cloud services from within a channel or chat. Each bot comes with either a library of set commands that you can invoke or the ability to parse natural language. Either way, you @mention the bot in a message, provide the query, and the bot handles all the hard background work of interfacing with its underlying cloud provider to provide you with either the information you seek or the service you request.

For example, using the Forms bot, you can construct a quick poll in a channel or chat by @mentioning Forms and then typing a question followed by each possible response, separated by commas.

5

 TIP You can tell bot messages from channel member messages by noting that member avatars are circles while bot avatars are hexagons.

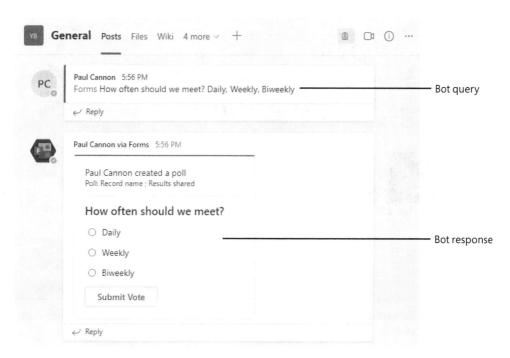

A Forms bot interaction in a channel

Install a bot

Teams gives you two ways to install a bot:

- **Via a channel or chat message** This is the most straightforward method because within the message, you can invoke the **Get bots** command, which displays a dialog showing all the available bots.

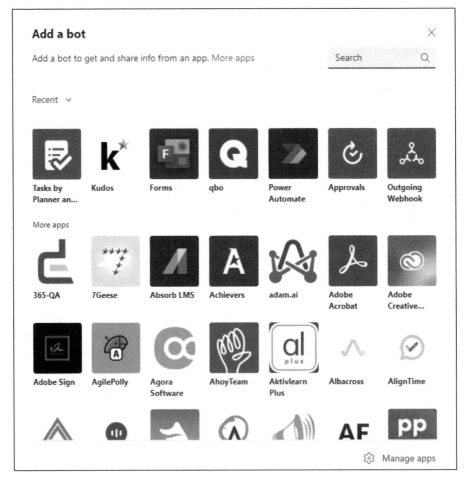

Selecting the Get Bots command in a chat or channel message displays this dialog that contains all the available bots.

- **Via the app store** This is the less straightforward method because the app store doesn't have a separate category for bots. One possibility is to perform a search on the term **bot**, which returns some—but, unfortunately, not all—of the apps that have a bot component. Alternatively, the only way to be sure that an app has a bot is to select the app in the app store. In the app's information window, look for a section named **Bots**.

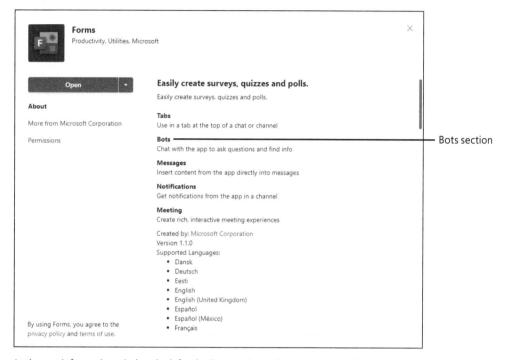

Bots section

In the app information window, look for the Bots section to know you're installing an app that has a bot component.

To install a bot from a channel or chat message

1. In the channel or chat where you want the bot to operate, start a new message.

2. Type @.

3. Select **Get bots** to open the **Add a Bot** dialog.

4. Select the bot you want to install. Teams displays the app's information window.

5. Select **Add**. Teams installs the bot.

To install a bot from the app store

1. Display the app store.

2. Select the app that contains the bot you want to install.

3. Select **Add to a team** or **Add to a chat**.

4. Type either the team and channel name or the chat name.

5. Select **Set up**. Teams install the app and adds the bot to the specified channel or chat.

Interact with a bot

To invoke a bot, you @mention the bot in a channel or chat message, and then type your query or request. When you type @ and then start typing the bot name, Teams displays a Suggestions list of matching items, including the bot you want to invoke. When you select the bot to complete the @mention, you then enter your command or query.

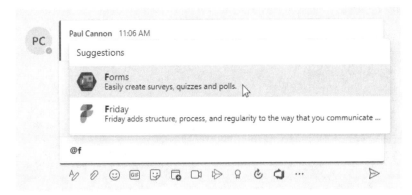

Enter @, start entering the bot name, and then select the bot from the Suggestions list.

Many bots display a Select or type a command link that, when selected, displays a menu that tells you what you can do with the bot. The menu content varies depending on the bot, but most include an example query, a Help command, and a command to use the app interface to create new content.

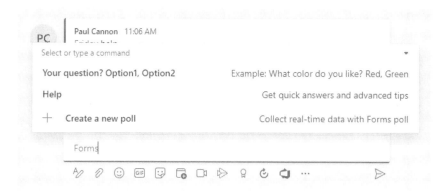

Select the Select or type a command link to display a menu of bot options

To invoke a bot

1. In the channel or chat where you installed the bot, start a new message.

2. Enter @, and then start entering the bot name.

3. When the bot name appears in the **Suggestions** list, select it.

4. Enter your bot query or command, and then select **Send**.

Key points

- Using apps in Teams helps you avoid some of the temporal and cognitive costs of task-switching by enabling you to perform many external tasks within the Teams interface.

- Teams offers a half dozen app types: personal apps, tabs, messaging extensions, meeting extensions, connectors, and bots.

- Some apps are developed by Microsoft, but most come from third-party developers. You can also create your own custom apps.

- You can access all Microsoft, third-party, and custom apps using the Teams app store.

- To display the app store, select the **Apps** icon in the app bar.

- To see a list of the apps you have installed, select the **More added apps** icon in the app bar.

Work with files

It's easy to think of Microsoft Teams as purely a communications platform given the myriad ways Teams offers to connect with people: chat, channel conversations, meetings, phone calls, and so on. But Teams is also big on collaboration, and the proof of that is the large collection of tools and features that Teams offers for working with files. For example, you can create, upload, and edit Microsoft 365 documents without leaving the Teams environment. And you can share those documents with channel members for a fully collaborative experience. And after you have files in Teams, you have access to a complete suite of file management tools.

This chapter guides you through procedures related to creating and uploading files and folders within a Teams channel. If you have files in another cloud storage provider, you also learn how to access those files within Teams. You also learn how to edit Microsoft 365 documents within Teams as well as within the browser or on the desktop. Finally, you also learn how to perform basic file management tasks such as renaming, moving, and deleting files, how to create custom folder views, and how to share a file or folder.

In this chapter

- Add files and folders
- Open and edit files
- Manage files and folders
- Customize the folder view

Add files and folders

Almost all teams require files of some kind, as well as folders to store them in. For example, a team working on a press release will need to create and work with a Word document. Similarly, another team working on a budget might need Excel files from each department as the raw budget data, as well as a new Excel workbook for the final budget.

In Teams, the fundamental storage medium for files is the channel. This makes sense because a channel is a team subset that's devoted to a particular topic, and storing files within the channel makes it easy for channel members to view and work with files related to that topic. (However, as you'll see later in this section, Teams also enables you to upload a file to a chat.)

Teams gives you three ways to add files and folders to a channel:

- **Create a new file or folder**   You can create new folders as well as new, blank Microsoft 365 files without leaving the Teams interface. You can create Word documents, Excel workbooks, and more.

- **Upload an existing file or folder**   If you already have a file or folder you want to use within Teams, you can upload it to a channel. You can upload using the Open dialog or you can drag and drop files and folders from File Explorer (Windows) or Finder (macOS).

- **Add a cloud storage folder**   If you have existing files in a folder with another cloud storage provider, such as SharePoint, Dropbox, or Google Drive (and you have permission to access that folder), you can add that folder to Teams.

Files and folders you create, upload, or add to Teams are stored in a channel's Files tab. Each Files tab is a front-end for a SharePoint library, and Teams gives you quick access to the channel's underlying SharePoint library in case you want to work with your files directly in SharePoint.

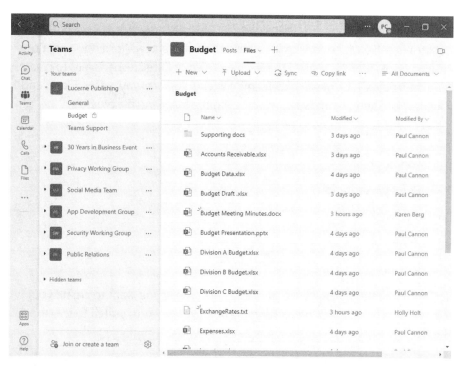

You access a channel's files and folders via the Files tab.

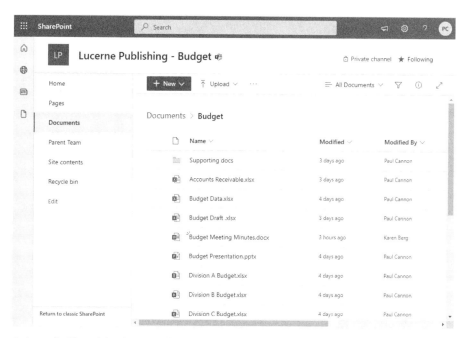

A channel's Files tab is a front-end for a SharePoint library.

Create files and folders in channels

If you require a new file while working in a channel, such as a new Word document or a new Excel workbook, there's no need to switch to Word or Excel, respectively, to create the file, and then upload the new file to Teams. Instead, you can stay within Teams and create your new file there. Teams supports creating the following file types:

- Word document
- Excel workbook
- PowerPoint presentation
- OneNote notebook
- Forms for Excel
- Visio drawing

Note that Teams creates a blank version of each file type. If you want to create your new file based on a template or an existing file, then you need to switch to the app to create the file.

Any user in a channel—an owner, a member, and even a guest—can create files and folders in the channel.

To create a file in the Files tab

1. Select the **Files** tab of the channel in which you want to create the file.

2. In the upper-left corner, select **New** to display a list of the objects you can create.

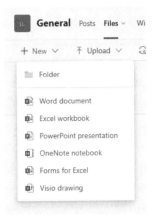

Select New to see a list of the file types that Teams can create.

3. Select the type of file you want to create.

4. When Teams prompts you to enter a name for the new file, enter the name you want to use for the file.

5. Select **Create**. Teams creates the file and opens it for editing using the associated app.

To create a folder in the Files tab

1. In the **Files** tab, select **New**, and then select **Folder**.

2. In the **Create a folder** dialog, enter the name you want to use for the folder, and then select **Create**.

Upload files and folders to channels

If the files or folders you need to use within a team channel are already on your computer, you can upload copies of those items to the channel and work with them within Teams.

 IMPORTANT Teams gives each organization 1 TB of storage space, and most Teams subscriptions also provide an extra 10 GB of storage for each license that you purchase.

Teams gives you four ways to upload a file or folder:

- **Dialog**   Enables you to use the Open dialog to choose the file you want to upload or the Select Folder dialog to choose the folder you want to upload

- **Drag and drop**   Enables you to use File Explorer (Windows) or Finder (macOS) to select the files or folders you want to upload, drag them into the Teams app, and then drop them inside a channel's Files tab

- **Channel message**   Enables you to initiate the Open dialog upload method from a channel message

- **Chat**   Enables you to upload a file to a chat conversation

 IMPORTANT The maximum size of a file you can upload to Teams is 250 GB.

Any channel user— an owner, a member, and even a guest—can upload files and folders to the channel.

To upload a file via the Open dialog

1. In the **Files** tab, select **Upload**, and then select **Files**.

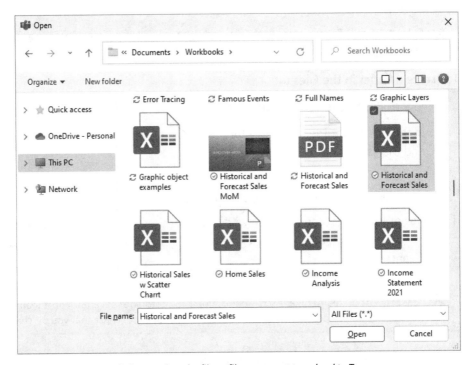

You can use the Open dialog to select the file or files you want to upload to Teams.

2. Select the location of the file you want to upload.

3. Select the file.

> **TIP** If you want to upload multiple files, hold down **Ctrl** (Windows) or **Cmd** (macOS) and select each file.

4. Select **Open**. Teams uploads the selected file.

To upload a folder via the Select Folder dialog

1. In the **Files** tab, select **Upload**.

2. In the **Open** dialog, select **Folder**.

3. In the **Select Folder** dialog, select the folder you want to upload, and then select the **Select Folder** button.

To upload a file or folder via drag and drop

1. Display the **Files** tab.

2. In File Explorer (Windows) or Finder (macOS), select the file or folder you want to upload and drag it to the **Files** tab of the Teams app.

> **TIP** If you want to upload multiple files or folders, hold down **Ctrl** (Windows) or **Cmd** (macOS) and select each item.

To upload a file to a channel message

1. In the **Posts** tab, start a new message or reply to an existing message.

2. Under the message box, select the **Attach** button.

3. Select **Upload from my computer**.

Attach icon

In a channel message, select the Attach button.

4. In the **Open** dialog, browse to and select the file you want to upload. Then select **Open**.

> **TIP** If you want to upload multiple files, hold down **Ctrl** (Windows) or **Cmd** (macOS) and select each file.

5. After Teams uploads the selected file, a file button appears within the message window. Complete your message and then select **Send**.

> **TIP** You or anyone viewing your channel message can select the file button to open the uploaded file for editing in Teams.

To upload a file to a chat

1. In the Chat Panel, select an existing chat or start a new one.

2. Below the message box, select the **Attach Files** button (the paperclip), and then select **OneDrive** or **Upload from my computer**.

3. In the **Open** dialog, browse to and select the file(s) you want to attach to the chat. Then select **Open**.

 TIP If you want to attach multiple files, hold down **Ctrl** (Windows) or **Cmd** (macOS) and select each file.

4. After Teams uploads the selected file, a file button appears within the chat window. Complete your message and then select **Send**.

 TIP You or anyone viewing your channel message can select the file button to open the uploaded file for editing in Teams.

Add cloud storage folders to channels

If the files you need to work with in a Teams channel are already stored in the cloud, you probably don't want duplicates of those files on Teams. To avoid that, you can give Teams permission to access the cloud storage folder in your channel.

Teams supports the following cloud storage providers:

- SharePoint
- Dropbox
- Box
- Egnyte
- ShareFile
- Google Drive

In each case, you must have the requisite authority on the storage provider to assign permission to Teams to access the folder.

> ⚠️ **IMPORTANT** The folder you work with in Teams is only a mirror of the original cloud storage folder. When you make changes to the folder or its files within Teams, you're really making changes to the original folder or its files.

To add a folder from another cloud storage provider

1. In the **Files** tab, select **Add cloud storage**.

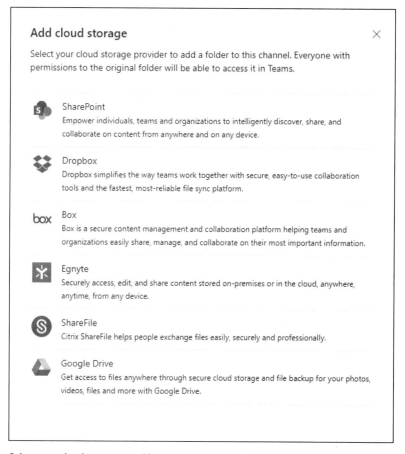

Select your cloud storage provider.

2. In the **Add cloud storage** dialog, select your cloud storage provider.

3. Follow the prompts to provide permission to Teams to access your storage on the provider. In most cases, you're asked to sign in to the provider and then select **Allow**.

4. Select the folder on the cloud storage provider you want to add to the channel, and then select **Add folder**.

Open and edit files

Almost any file that you can upload to Teams you can also open in Teams for viewing. This is convenient and efficient when all you want to do is preview the contents of a file, and it can be a lifesaver if you don't own a copy of the file's associated application.

File types supported by Teams

Although you can only edit Microsoft 365 files in Teams, you can open hundreds of file types for viewing without requiring the associated application. Here's a list of file types supported by Teams as of this writing:

File type	File extension(s)
3-D Modeling and printing	.3mf, .cool, .glb, .gltf, .obj, .stl
Apple	.movie, .pages, .pict, .sketch
Adobe	.ai, .pdf, .psb, .psd
Audio/video media files	.3g2, .3gp, .3gpp, .asf, .avi, .m2ts, .m4a, .m4v, .mkv, .mov, .mp3, .mp4, .mp4v, .mts, .ts, .wav, .webm, .wma, .wmv
AutoCAD	.dwg
Autodesk	.fbx
BioWare Game Engine	.erf
Compressed file	.zip
Compressed file (Unix)	.z
DICOM medical images	.dcm, .dcm30, .dicm, .dicom
Finale	.ply
HydroCAD	.hcp

File type	File extension(s)
Image formats	.gif, .heic, .heif, .jpeg, .jpg, .jpe, .mef, .mrw, .nef, .nrw, .orf, .pano, .pef, .png, .rw2, .spm, .tif, .tiff, .xbm, .xcf
License key	.key
Log file	.log
Microsoft 365 (Excel, PowerPoint, Word)	.csv, .dic, .doc, .docm, .docx, .dotm, .dotx, .pot, .potm, .potx, .pps, .ppsm, .ppsx, .ppt, .pptm, .pptx, .xd, .xls, .xlsb, .xlsx, .sltx
Microsoft Outlook	.eml, .msg
Microsoft Visio	.vsd, .vsdx
Microsoft Windows	.cur, .ico, .icon
Open eBook	.epub
OpenOffice	.odp, .ods, .odt
Photo	.arw, .cr2, .crw, .dng
Rich Text Format	.rtf
Text and code	.abap, .ada, .adp, .ahk, .as, .as3, .asc, .ascx, .asm, .asp, .awk, .bas, .bash, .bash_login, .bash_logout, .bash_profile, .bashrc, .bat, .bib, .bsh, .build, .builder, .c, .c++, .capfile, .cbk, .cc, .cfc, .cfm, .cfml, .cl, .clj, .cmake, .cmd, .coffee, .cpp, .cpt, .cpy, .cs, .cshtml, .cson, .csproj, .css, .ctp, .cxx, .d, .ddl, .di, .dif, .diff, .disco, .dml, .dtd, .dtml, .el, .emake, .erb, .erl, .f90, .f95, .fs, .fsi, .fsscript, .fsx, .gemfile, .gemspec, .gitconfig, .go, .groovy, .gvy, .h, .h++, .haml, .handlebars, .hbs, .hrl, .hs, .htc, .html, .hxx, .idl, .iim, .inc, .inf, .ini, .inl, .ipp, .irbrc, .jade, .jav, .java, .js, .json, .jsp, .jsx, .l, .less, .lhs, .lisp, .log, .lst, .ltx, .lua, .m, .make, .markdn, .markdown, .md, .mdown, .mkdn, .ml, .mli, .mll, .mly, .mm, .mud, .nfo, .opml, .osascript, .out, .p, .pas, .patch, .php, .php2, .php3, .php4, .php5, .pl, .plist, .pm, .pod, .pp, .profile, .properties, .ps, .ps1, .pt, .py, .pyw, .r, .rake, .rb, .rbx, .rc, .re, .readme, .reg, .rest, .resw, .resx, .rhtml, .rjs, .rprofile, .rpy, .rss, .rst, .rxml, .s, .sass, .scala, .scm, .sconscript, .sconstruct, .script, .scss, .sgml, .sh, .shtml, .sml, .sql, .sty, .tcl, .tex, .text, .textile, .tld, .tli, .tmpl, .tpl, .txt, .vb, .vi, .vim, .wsdl, .xaml, .xhtml, .xoml, .xml, .xsd, .xsl, .xslt, .yaml, .yaws, .yml, .zsh
Web and hypertext	.htm, .html, .markdown, .md, .url

6

One of the great conveniences of Teams is that you can work with Excel, PowerPoint, and Word files within Teams itself. In most cases, there's no need to switch to the associated desktop app to edit a document. The exceptions are when you need a more advanced app feature because the Teams version of each Microsoft 365 app supports only a subset of the features of the corresponding desktop app.

When you select an Excel, PowerPoint, or Word file within Teams, the default behavior is to open the file in the Teams window, but you can also view or edit the file in your default web browser or in the file's associated desktop app. You can also change the default to open Excel, PowerPoint, and Word files in the browser rather than in Teams.

To open a file

- In the channel where the file is stored, select the **Files** tab and then select the file.

- Select **Files** in the app bar to display the **Files** panel, select **Microsoft Teams** (or select **Recent** if the file is one that was recently created, uploaded, or modified), and then select the file.

- In the Teams **Search** box, type /files and press **Enter** or **Return** to display a list of recently used files, and then select the file you want to view.

- In a channel or chat message with an attached file, select the file's button in the message.

To close an open file

- In the upper-right corner of the preview window, select **Close** (×).

- In the upper-left corner of the preview window, select **Back** (<).

> **TIP** To jump directly to a recent channel or file, hover the mouse pointer over **Back** (<) and then select the channel or file from the list that appears.

Back

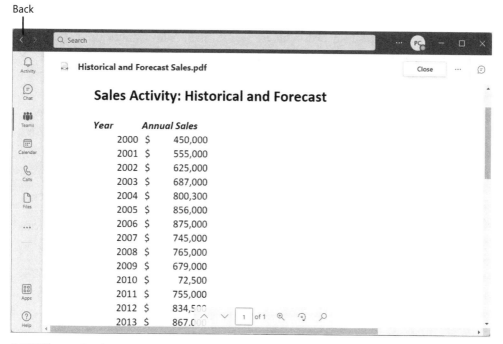

A PDF file open for viewing in Teams

To edit a Word, PowerPoint, or Excel file in Teams

▪ In the **Files** tab, select the file to open it for editing.

To edit a Word, PowerPoint, or Excel file in the web browser

▪ In the **Files** tab, right-click the file (or select the file's **Show actions** (...) button), select **Open**, and then select **Open in browser** to open the file for editing in the associated Microsoft 365 web app in your default web browser.

To edit a Word, PowerPoint, or Excel file in the associated Microsoft 365 desktop app

- In the **Files** tab, right-click the file (or select the file's **Show actions (...)** button), select **Open**, and then select **Open in app** to open the file for editing in the associated Microsoft 365 desktop app.

- With the file open for editing in Teams, select **Open in Desktop App**.

- With the file open for editing in the web browser, select **Editing**, and then select **Open in Desktop App**.

To change the default opening behavior for Word, PowerPoint, and Excel files

1. Select the **Files** tab of a channel that contains a Word, PowerPoint, or Excel file.

2. Right-click any Word, PowerPoint, or Excel file (or select the file's **Show actions** (...) button), select **Open**, and then select **Change default**.

3. In the **Change default** dialog, select your preferred option for opening Word, PowerPoint, and Excel files (**Teams** or **Browser**), and then select **Save**.

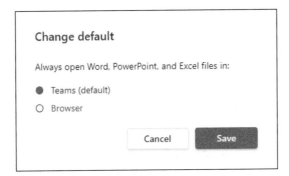

In the Change default dialog, set the default for how you want to open Excel, PowerPoint, and Word files.

Manage files and folders

If you do a lot of work with files in Teams, you'll appreciate the extensive collection of file management tools that teams offers. In a channel's Files tab, each file or folder has an Actions menu that contains all the available management commands.

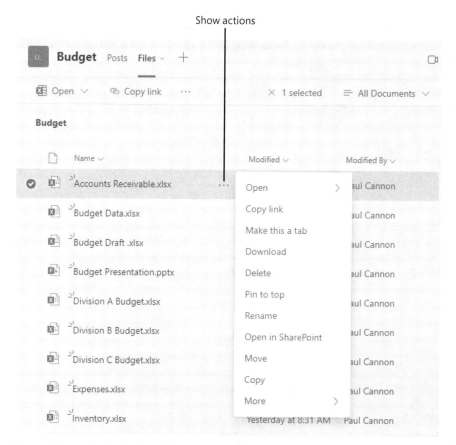

Teams offers a robust collection of file management tools.

The items in the Actions menu vary slightly depending on the file type, but they usually include the following commands:

- **Copy link**   Copies a link to a file or folder to the Clipboard.

- **Make this a tab**   Creates a tab in the channel for a Word, PowerPoint, or Excel file. Selecting the tab opens the file for editing in that tab.

- **Download**   Downloads the file or folder to your computer.

- **Delete**   Removes the file or folder from the channel.

- **Pin to top**   Displays a file or folder at the top of the Files tab for easy access. For a pinned folder, Teams uses a folder icon; for a pinned file, Teams uses a thumbnail image of the file.

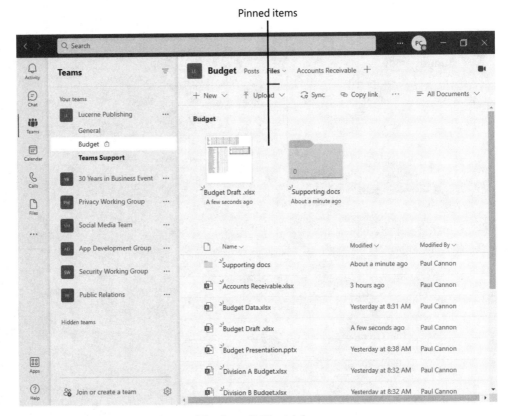

You can pin files and folders to the top of the channel's Files tab for easy access.

- **Rename**   Changes the name of a file or folder.

- **Open in SharePoint**   Displays the SharePoint library that contains the file or folder.

- **Move**   Moves a file (but not a folder) to another folder in the same channel, a different channel in the same team, or a channel in a different team. You can also move the file to a location on OneDrive or any cloud storage provider you've added to Teams (such as Dropbox or Google Drive).

- **Copy**   Copies a file (but not a folder) to another folder in the same channel, a different channel in the same team, or a channel in a different team. You can also copy the file to a location on OneDrive or any cloud storage provider you've added to Teams (such as Dropbox or Google Drive).

- **More**   Displays a fly-out menu that contains the Check out command, which is used to reserve a file so that no other channel member can open the file. However, Teams is designed for collaboration on files, so using the Check out command is considered bad practice and should be avoided.

To pin a file or folder to the top of the Files tab

- In the **Files** tab, right-click the file or folder (or select the file or folder's **Show actions (…)** button), and then select **Pin to top**.

 IMPORTANT   You can pin a maximum of three items.

 TIP   You can move a pinned file or folder: right-click the pinned item, select **Edit pin**, and then select **Move left** or **Move right**.

 TIP   To remove a pinned item, right-click it, select **Edit pin**, and then select **Unpin**.

To rename a file or folder

1. In the **Files** tab, right-click the file or folder (or select the file or folder's **Show actions (…)** button), and then select **Rename**.

2. In the **Rename** dialog, enter the new name and then select **Save**.

To download a file or folder

1. In the **Files** tab, right -click the file or folder (or select the file or folder's **Show actions (…)** button), and then select **Download**.

2. In the **Download** dialog, browse to the location in which you want to save the file or the zipped folder.

3. If you want to, you can edit the file name.

4. Select **Save**.

TIP To download multiple files and/or folders, select the checkbox to the left of each item you want to download, and then select **Download** in the **Files** tab toolbar.

 TIP To see your completed and in-progress downloads, select **Files** in the app bar to open the **Files** Panel, and then select **Downloads**. On this screen, you can also select **Open Downloads Folder** to view your computer's Downloads folder in File Explorer (Windows) or Finder (macOS).

To delete a file or folder

1. In the **Files** tab, right-click the file or folder (or select the file or folder's **Show actions (...)** button), and then select **Delete**.

2. In the **Delete?** dialog, select **Delete**.

> **TIP** To delete multiple files and/or folders, select the checkbox to the left of each item you want to delete, and then select **Delete** in the **Files** tab toolbar.

To display the SharePoint library behind a channel File tab

- At the right end of the **Files** tab, select **Open in SharePoint**.

To make a file available as a tab

1. In the **Files** tab, right-click the file (or select the file's **Show actions (...)** button), and then select **Make this a tab**.

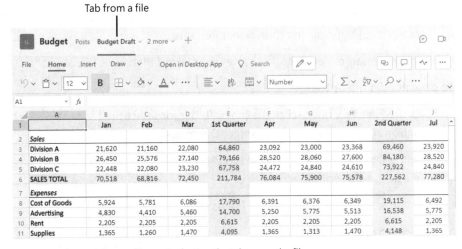

You can make a tab from a file, and selecting the tab opens the file.

To copy a file to another location within Teams

1. In the **Files** tab, right-click the file (or select the file's **Show actions** (**...**) button), and then select **Copy**.

2. In the **Copy to** dialog, select the location to which you want to copy the file, and then select **Copy**.

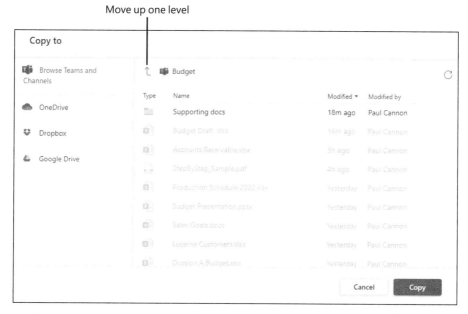

Use the Copy to dialog to select a location for your copied file.

To move a file to another location within Teams

1. In the **Files** tab, right-click the file (or select the file's **Show actions** (**...**) button), and then select **Move**.

2. In the **Move to** dialog, select the location to which you want to move the file, and then select **Move**.

To share a link to a file or folder

1. In the **Files** tab, right-click the file or folder (or select the file or folder's **Show actions (...)** button), and then select **Copy link**. Teams copies a link to the file or folder to the Clipboard.

2. To specify who the link should work for, follow these steps:

   a. Select the **People in your organization with the link can edit** link to open the Link Settings dialog.

   b. Select an option for who you want the link to work for: **People in your organization with the link**, **People with existing access**, or **Specific people**. If you select **Specific people**, use the text box to enter their names or email addresses.

   c. If you don't want people to edit the file or folder, clear the **Allow editing** checkbox.

   d. Select **Apply**. Teams generates a new link based on the changed settings.

   e. Select **Copy**.

3. Share the copied link with the person or people you want to have access to the file or folder.

Customize the folder view

By default, each channel's Files tab shows a list of all the available files, with four columns of data about each file:

- **Type**   Displays an icon that represents the file type of each item in the list.

- **Name**   Displays the name of the file or folder.

- **Modified**   Displays the amount of time since the file or folder was created, uploaded, or last edited.

- **Modified By**   Displays the name of the channel member who created, uploaded, or last edited the file.

In this default view, which is called *All Documents*, the items are sorted by the contents of the Name column, with folders at the top. However, Teams offers an extensive set of features for customizing the view, including the following:

- **Change the display**   Show the folders and files as the default list; as a compact list (that is, a list with less vertical space between each item); and as tiles (that is, a collection of thumbnails that display a preview of the contents of each file and the Name and Modified By data for each file).

- **Sort**   Order the files and folders based on the contents of a column.

- **Filter**   Display a subset of the files and folders by selecting one or more unique values from a column.

- **Group**   Display the files and folders grouped according to the unique values in a column.

- **Edit in SharePoint**   Open the view in SharePoint, which enables you to modify the following aspects of the view:

  - **View Name**   Edit the name of the view.

  - **Columns**   Choose the columns to display in the view and each column's position in the view. SharePoint offers more than 30 columns, including Content Type, File Size, and Version.

  - **Sort**   Order the items based on the contents of up to two columns.

  - **Filter**   Display a subset of the items based on the unique values in two or more columns. If you specify multiple columns, you can apply the filter when all column criteria are true or when at least one of the column criteria is true.

  - **Tabular View**   Toggle item checkboxes on and off. Members use these checkboxes to select one or more items in the view.

  - **Group By**   Group the items based on the contents of up to two columns.

  - **Totals**   Display a total at the bottom of the column. Here, "total" refers to any mathematical operator applied to the column. The available operators depend on the content type of the column, but include the following: Sum, Count, Average, Maximum, and Minimum.

  - **Style**   Apply a predefined style to the list.

6

- **Folders**   Choose whether to display items inside their folders or without their folders.

- **Item Limit**   Set the total number of items to show at a time.

- **Mobile**   Enable the view for mobile users.

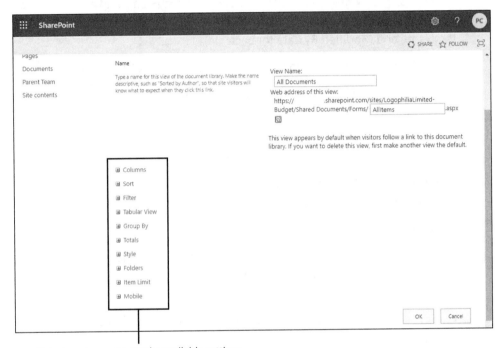

Select a category to see the available settings

You can edit a Files tab view in SharePoint.

You're not limited to only modifying the All Documents view. You can also save your custom view as a new view, and you can create new views from scratch in SharePoint.

> ⚠️ **IMPORTANT**   When you make changes to the view in Teams, those changes are temporary and last only as long as the current Files tab session. That is, if you navigate away from the Files tab and then return to it, Teams redisplays the default view. If you want to make your view modifications permanent, either save the view as a new view or make your view modifications in SharePoint.

To change the display of files and folders in the Files tab

■ In the upper-right corner of the **Files** tab, select **Switch view options**, and then select a view: **List**, **Compact List**, or **Tiles**.

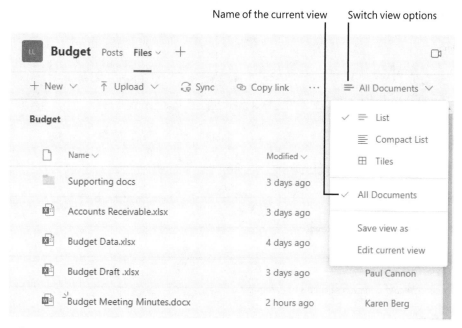

Select Switch View Options to change the current Files tab view.

To sort files

■ In the **Files** tab, select the header of the column on which you want to base the sort, and then select a sort command, the name of which depends on the content type of the column:

- **Icon**   Select either **Ascending** or **Descending**.

- **Text**   Select either **A to Z** or **Z to A**.

- **Numeric**   Select either **Smaller to larger** or **Larger to smaller**.

- **Date or time**   Select either **Older to newer** or **Newer to older**.

Column header

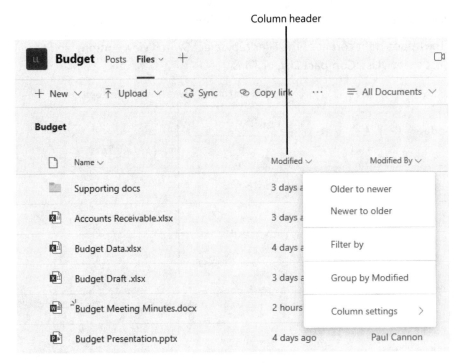

Select a column header and then select a sort command.

To filter files

1. In the **Files** tab, select the header of the column that contains the unique values you want to use as the basis of the filter, and then select **Filter by**.

2. In the **Filter by '*Column*'** pane, select the checkbox beside each unique value you want to see in the filtered view, and then select **Apply**.

 TIP To remove the filter, repeat the process, but in step 2, select **Clear all**, and then select **Apply**.

Select each unique value that you want to include in the filtered view.

To group files

- In the **Files** tab, select the header of the column that contains the unique values you want to use as groupings, and then select **Group by** *Column* (where *Column* is the name of the column you selected). Teams groups the files and folders based on the unique values in the selected column.

To save a custom view

1. In the **Files** tab, modify the view, sorting, filtering, and grouping as you want them in your custom view.

2. In the upper-right corner, select **Switch view options**, and then select **Save view as**.

3. In the **Save as** dialog, enter a name for the new view.

4. If you don't want this view to be available to other channel members, clear the **Make this a public view** checkbox.

5. Select **Save**.

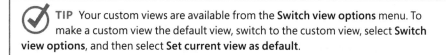

TIP Your custom views are available from the **Switch view options** menu. To make a custom view the default view, switch to the custom view, select **Switch view options**, and then select **Set current view as default**.

To edit a view in SharePoint

1. Display the view you want to edit.

2. In the upper-right corner of the **Files** tab, select **Switch view options**, and then select **Edit current view** to open the view in SharePoint.

3. Use the SharePoint controls to modify the view as needed, and then select **OK**.

4. In Teams, select the **Tab options** button for the **Files** tab, and then select **Reload tab** to reload the default view.

5. If you edited a view other than the default, select **Switch view options** and then select the edited view.

To delete a custom view

1. Display the view you want to delete.

2. In the upper-right corner of the **Files** tab, select **Switch view options**, and then select **Edit current view** to open the view in SharePoint.

3. At the top of the page, select **Delete**. SharePoint asks you to confirm.

4. Select **OK**.

5. In Teams, select the **Tab options** button for the **Files** tab and then select **Reload tab** to reload the default view.

To create a new view in SharePoint

1. In the upper-right corner of the **Files** tab, select **Switch view options**, and then select **Edit current view** to open the Edit View page in SharePoint.

2. Without making any changes, in the upper-right corner, select **OK** to display the SharePoint library for the current **Files** tab.

3. In SharePoint, select **Switch view options**, and then select **Create new view**.

4. In the **Create view** dialog, do the following:

   - Enter a view name.

   - Select the view type: **List**, **Calendar**, or **Gallery**.

   - If you want the view to be private, clear the **Make this a public view** checkbox.

5. Select **Create** to switch to the new view in SharePoint.

6. Select **Switch view options**, and then select **Edit current view**.

7. Use the SharePoint controls to modify the view as needed, and then select **OK**.

8. In Teams, select the **Tab options** button for the **Files** tab and then select **Reload tab** to reload the default view.

9. Select **Switch view options**, and then select the new view.

Key points

- In Teams, you almost always work with files within a channel.

- To add a file or folder to a channel, you can create it within Teams, upload it to Teams from your computer, or add a storage folder from a cloud service provider to Teams.

- To access your files, navigate to the channel and select the Files tab, which is a front-end for a SharePoint library where the files are stored online.

- From within Teams, you can create Word documents, Excel workbooks, PowerPoint presentations, OneNote notebooks, Forms for Excel, and Visio drawings.

- You can edit Excel, PowerPoint, and Word files within Teams.

- If you make changes to a Files tab's view in SharePoint, you need to refresh the view in Teams by reloading the Files tab.

6

Chat with members of your team

With the business and enterprise versions of Teams, channel conversations (see Chapter 4, "Converse in a channel") are one of the main ways that team members stay in touch and resolve important issues. However, a channel conversation isn't always the best way to communicate in Teams. For one thing, you can't be sure that a team member sees an important channel message right away because that person might have turned off notifications for that channel. For another, many team issues that arise require a conversation with just one other person, or perhaps two or three others. To hash out that issue in front of a couple of dozen channel members is inefficient and a waste of time for the people not involved in the issue.

For these and similar situations, a chat is a better way to communicate. Chats are designed for one-on-one and small-group conversations. Chat participants always receive notification of new messages.

This chapter guides you through procedures related to managing contacts and contact groups, chatting with one or more people, enhancing chat messages, and managing chat messages.

In this chapter

- Manage contacts and contact groups
- Chat with one or more people
- Enhance chat messages
- Manage chat messages

Manage contacts and contact groups

Teams doesn't have a separate "contacts" app. Instead, everyone in your organization has a contact card that shows the person's availability status, current time (and time zone, if it differs from yours), and email address, as well as several options for interacting with the person (such as starting a chat, a video call, or a voice call).

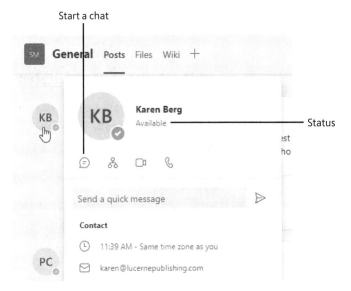

A team member's contact card

However, Teams does offer a Contacts section in the Chat Panel. In that section, you perform three tasks:

- **Add contacts to your Favorites**   If you're part of a large team but have just a few people you chat with regularly, adding them to your Favorites group makes it easier to initiate chats with those members.

- **Create contact groups**   If you regularly chat with two or more team members, you can create a group consisting of those contacts. You can then specify the group name when starting a chart with those members.

- **Notify you when a contact becomes available**   If you want to chat with someone, but that person's current status is Away, Busy, or otherwise unavailable, you can ask Teams to send you a notification when that contact's status changes to Available.

> ⚠️ **IMPORTANT** If you're using Teams on a mobile device, you work with contacts by giving Teams access to your device's Contacts list. On Android, open Settings, select **Privacy**, select **Permission Manager**, select **Contacts**, select **Teams**, and then select **Allow**. On iOS or iPadOS, open **Settings**, select **Privacy**, select **Contacts**, and then select the **Teams** switch to turn it **On**.

To view someone's contact card

- If the person has posted to a channel, display that channel's **Posts** tab, and then select the person's avatar.

- If the person has taken part in a chat, select **Chat** in the app bar to open the Chat Panel, and then select the person's avatar.

- If the person has performed any Teams action that is part of your feed, select **Activity** in the app bar to open the Feed Panel, and then select the person's avatar.

To add a contact to your Favorites group (desktop and web apps only)

1. In the app bar, select **Chat**.

2. At the top of the Chat Panel, select the **Chat** heading to display the menu, and then select **Contacts**.

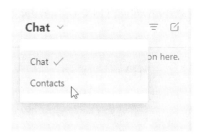

Switching to the Contacts section of the Chat panel

3. To the right of the **Favorites** group heading, select **More options (...)**, and then select **Add a contact to this group**.

4. In the **Add to Contacts** dialog, start typing the name of the person you want to add. When the person's name appears in the search results, select it, and then select **Add**.

To create a contact group (desktop and web apps only)

1. At the bottom of the Contacts Panel, select **Create a new contact group**.

2. In the **Create a New Contact Group** dialog, in the **Contact group name** text box, enter a name for the group.

3. Select **Create**.

To add a contact to a contact group (desktop and web apps only)

1. In the Contacts Panel, to the right of the group name, select **More options** (…), and then select **Add a contact to this group**.

2. In the **Add to Contacts** dialog, start typing the name of the person you want to add. When the person's name appears in the search results, select it and then select **Add**.

To remove a contact from a group (desktop and web apps only)

- In the Contacts Panel, in the group from which you want to remove the contact, select **More options** (…) to the right of the contact's name, and then select **Remove from this group**.

To get a notification when a contact becomes available (desktop and web apps only)

- In the Contacts Panel, in the Favorites list or any contact group, to the right of the contact's name, select **More options** (…), and then select **Notify when available**.

Chat with one or more people

There are four ways you can chat with people:

- **Private chat**   A chat between you and one other person
- **Quick message**   A brief chat message sent to one person
- **Group chat**   A chat between you and two or more other people
- **Pop-out chat**   A private or group chat that takes place in a separate window

When you create a new chat, Teams names the chat after the person (in the case of a private chat or quick message) or people (in the case of a group chat) you're chatting with. However, you're free to rename the chat to something more relevant to the discussion.

The name you give to a chat appears at the top of the chat area, to the left of the chat tabs. Of these tabs, the chat messages themselves appear in the Chat tab. If you upload files in the chat, you work with these files in the Files tab.

To initiate a private or group chat

- In the app bar, select **Chat**, and then, in the upper-right corner of the Chat Panel, select **New Chat**. (In Android, the New Chat button appears in the lower-right corner of the Chat Panel.)

- From anywhere in the Teams desktop app, press **Ctrl+N** (Windows) or **Cmd+N** (macOS).

- Display the contact card for the person you want to chat with, and then select the **Start a chat** button.

To create a private chat

1. Initiate the chat.

2. In the **To** field, start typing the name of the person you want to chat with. When the person's name appears in the search results, select it.

3. Enter your message in the compose box at the bottom of the screen.

4. Select **Send** or press **Enter** or **Return**.

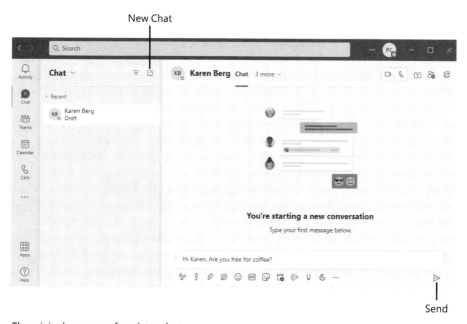

The original message of a private chat

Or

1. Display the contact card for the person with whom you want to chat.

2. In the **Send a quick message** text box, enter your message.

3. Select **Send** or press **Enter** or **Return**.

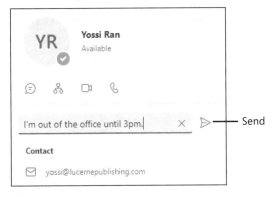

Initiate a chat message from a contact card

To create a group chat

1. Initiate the chat.

2. In the **To** field, start typing the name of one person you want to chat with. When the person's name appears in the search results, select it.

3. Repeat step 2 for each person you want in the chat.

Setting up a group chat

4. (Optional) To name the group chat, select **Add group name**, and then enter the name in the **Group name** field.

5. Enter your message in the compose box at the bottom of the screen.

6. Select **Send** or press **Enter** or **Return**.

To pop out a chat (desktop app only)

1. Select the chat.

2. Do either of the following:

   • In the Chat Panel, select **More options** (…) to the right of the chat name and then select **Pop out chat**.

   • Select the **Pop out chat** button, either to the right of the chat name or in the top-right corner of the chat.

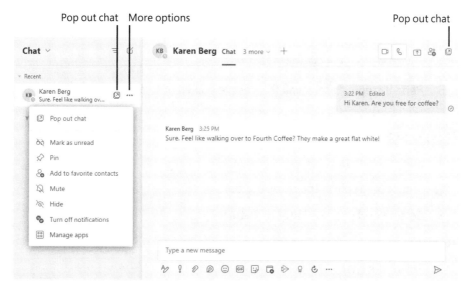

Select the Pop out chat command or button to pop out a chat to its own window.

To add people to a chat

1. Select the chat.

2. In the upper-right corner of the Teams window, select the **Add people** button.

3. If your chat is already a group chat, you see a menu of the people in the chat. At the bottom of that menu, select **Add people**.

> ⚠ **IMPORTANT** If you add people to an existing private chat, Teams creates a new group chat.

4. Start typing the name of a person you want to add to the chat. When the person's name appears in the search results, select it.

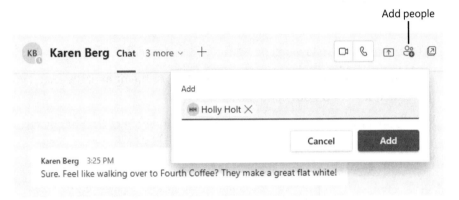

Select Add people to include more people in a chat.

5. Repeat step 4 to select all the people you want to add to the chat, and then select **Add**.

To reply to a chat message

1. Select the chat.

2. Enter your reply in the compose box.

3. Select **Send** or press **Enter** or **Return**.

To rename a group chat

1. Select the chat.

2. Do either of the following to open the chat name for editing:

   - **Desktop or web** To the right of the current chat name, select the **Name group chat** button.

   - **Mobile** Select the current chat name and then select **Name group chat** (Android) or **Group chat name** (iOS or iPadOS).

3. Enter the new name in the text box.

4. Select **Save** or **OK** (Android app only).

Name group chat

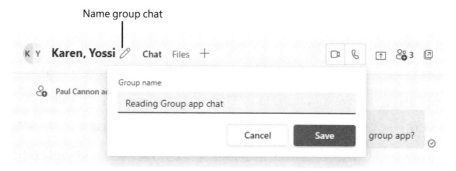

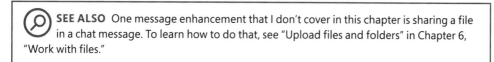

Select the chat's Name group chat button to rename the chat.

7

Enhance chat messages

Chat messages are meant to be simple exchanges between either one other person (a private chat) or a few other people (a group chat). Almost all chat conversations are quick exchanges of information, so the messages themselves are usually plain: unformatted text with no special features.

However, that doesn't mean you can't enhance your chat text if you think the enhancement will help get your message across or make your message more fun. To that end, Teams lets you apply a wide range of text formatting and offers special features such as emojis and animated GIFs.

> **SEE ALSO** One message enhancement that I don't cover in this chapter is sharing a file in a chat message. To learn how to do that, see "Upload files and folders" in Chapter 6, "Work with files."

> **IMPORTANT** Teams offers a rich array of tools to format and spice up your chat messages. That said, you don't want to throw everything into your messages because the result will almost certainly be unreadable. Add just enough enhancements to strengthen your message or add a bit of entertainment value but avoid unneeded extras that detract from your message.

Format chat message text

Whether you're composing an original chat message or replying to an existing message, you start out with a basic compose box. Although this text box presents no formatting controls, if you're using the Teams desktop or web app, you can still format selected message text as follows:

- Press **Ctrl+B** (Windows) or **Cmd+B** (macOS) to make the selected text bold.

- Press **Ctrl+I** (Windows) or **Cmd+I** (macOS) to make the selected text italic.

- Press **Ctrl+U** (Windows) or **Cmd+U** (macOS) to make the selected text underlined.

However, if you want to format your message text, it's usually faster and easier to display the formatting options, which include a toolbar with various formatting controls. (In the Teams desktop and web apps, you also get an expanded compose box.)

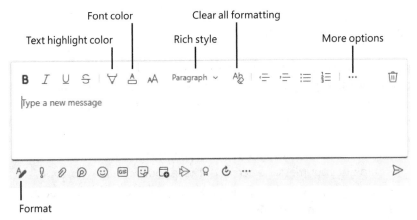

The text formatting options in the expanded chat message compose box

The formatting toolbar at the top of the expanded compose box offers the following formatting controls:

- **Bold**   Applies and removes bold formatting.

- **Italic**   Applies and removes italic formatting.

- **Underline**   Applies and removes underlining.

- **Strikethrough**   Applies and removes strikethrough formatting.

- **Text highlight color**   Displays a palette so you can select a text background color.

- **Font color**   Displays a palette so you can select a text color.

- **Font size**   Displays a list from which you can choose the text size: Large, Medium, or Small.

- **Rich style**   Displays a list from which you can apply a text style: Heading 1, Heading 2, Heading 3, Paragraph (that is, regular text), or Monospaced.

- **Clear all formatting**   Returns the selected text to the default Paragraph style by removing all formatting applied to the text.

- **More options**   Displays a menu of options for enhancing text, most of which I cover in the next section, "Structure chat message content." If your screen uses a wide resolution, you might not see the More options button; instead, all the buttons will appear in the expanded compose box toolbar.

> **TIP** Usually, you apply the formatting options to selected text. However, if you want to apply some formatting to the next text you type, position the insertion point where you want to start typing and then select the formatting you want to apply.

7

To expand a compose box and display the formatting toolbar

- At the left end of the button bar below the compose box, select the **Format** button.

- Press **Ctrl+Shift+X** (Windows) or **Cmd+Shift+X** (macOS)

- In the mobile app, select the **Add** (+) button to the left of the compose box, and then select **Format**.

To format chat message text

1. Expand the compose box of an unsent chat message to display the formatting toolbar.

2. Select the text you want to format or position the insertion point where you want to apply the formatting to text you're about to type.

3. Use the toolbar controls to apply the formatting.

4. (Desktop or web app only) If you're typing formatted text and you want the next text you type to have no formatting, select the **Clear all formatting** button in the toolbar.

Structure chat message content

Most chat messages are simple declarations, announcements, questions, or answers, so there's no need to provide any structure to the text. However, you'll certainly come across situations where applying some structure to your text will make it easier to understand. If you're using the Teams desktop or web app, you have quite a few options for adding structure to a chat message.

For example, if you're providing someone with instructions to perform a task, those instructions will be easier to follow if you structure them as a numbered list of steps. Similarly, if you're providing someone with some programming code, structuring that code as a code snippet will make it easier to read.

Here's a summary of the structural changes you can make to the content of a chat message (again, remember that these are only available with the Teams desktop and web apps):

- **Indent text**   Increasing the indent shifts the left edge of the current paragraph to the right; similarly, decreasing the indent shifts the left edge of the current paragraph to the left.

- **Bulleted list**   Arranges the selected text as a list of items, where each item is a paragraph from the selected text and each item is preceded by a bullet (a small, black dot).

- **Numbered list**   Arranges the selected text as a numbered sequence of items, where each item is a paragraph from the selected text and each item is preceded by a number, where the first paragraph is 1, the second paragraph is 2, and so on.

- **Quoted text**   Displays the selected paragraph indented with a light gray background and a dark gray left border. Use this structure if you want to include in your message a quotation from another person or work.

- **Link**   Converts text into a link to a web page, a file, or some other resource.

- **Code snippet**   Inserts one or more lines of code, where the text is in a monospace font with a light gray background and each line is numbered.

- **Horizontal rule**   Inserts a gray, horizontal line across the width of the compose box. Use horizontal rules to separate sections of your message.

- **Table**   Organizes text into a row-and-column format.

These message options are available from the compose box toolbar, which you display by selecting the Format button in an original message or a reply. Note that, depending on your screen resolution width, you might have to select the toolbar's More options button (...) to see some or all of the options.

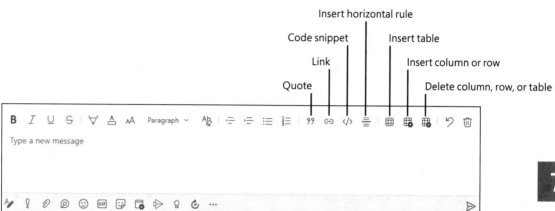

The message structure options in the chat message compose box

To increase the indent of text in a chat message

1. Do either of the following to select the text you want to indent

   - If you're indenting one paragraph, place the insertion point anywhere in the paragraph.

   - If you're indenting two or more paragraphs, select at least one character in each paragraph.

2. On the formatting toolbar, select **Increase indent**.

3. Repeat Step 2 until the text is indented as much as you want.

To decrease the indent of text in a chat message

1. Do either of the following to select the text for which you want to decrease the indent:

   - If you're working with one paragraph, place the insertion point anywhere in the paragraph.

   - If you're working with two or more paragraphs, select at least one character in each paragraph.

2. On the formatting toolbar, select **Decrease indent**.

3. Repeat Step 2 until the text indentation is decreased as much as you want.

To add a bulleted list to a chat message

1. Position the insertion point where you want the bulleted list to appear. If you want to convert existing text to a bulleted list, select that text.

2. On the formatting toolbar, select **Bulleted list**. If you converted existing text to a bulleted list and you want to add more items, position the insertion point at the end of the last item and skip to Step 4.

3. Type your item text.

4. Press **Enter** or **Return**. Teams adds a new item to the bulleted list.

5. Repeat Steps 3 and 4 until your bulleted list is complete.

6. In the final (empty) item, press **Enter** or **Return** a second time to complete the bulleted list.

To add a numbered list to a chat message

1. Position the insertion point where you want the numbered list to appear. If you want to convert existing text to a numbered list, select that text.

2. On the formatting toolbar, select **Numbered list**. If you converted existing text to a numbered list and you want to add more items, position the insertion point at the end of the last item and skip to Step 4.

3. Type the item text.

4. Press **Enter** or **Return**. Teams adds a new item to the numbered list.

5. Repeat Steps 3 and 4 until your numbered list is complete.

6. In the final (empty) item, press **Enter** or **Return** a second time to complete the numbered list.

To add quoted text to a chat message

1. Position the insertion point where you want the quotation to appear. If you want to convert existing text to a quotation, select that text.

2. On the formatting toolbar, select **Quote**. If you converted existing text to a quotation, you're done.

3. Type or paste the quotation text.

To add a link to a chat message

1. Select the text that you want to convert to a link.

2. On the formatting toolbar, select **Link** to display the Insert link dialog.

3. Edit the link text in the **Text to display** box, if necessary.

4. Type or paste the link address in the **Address** text box, and then select **Insert**.

Add a link to a chat message

To add a code snippet to a chat message

1. Position the insertion point where you want the code snippet to appear in your chat message.

2. On the formatting toolbar, select **Code snippet** to display the code snippet dialog.

3. Enter a title for the code.

4. From the list in the upper-right corner, select the type of code you're adding.

5. Enter your code in the large text box, and then select **Insert**.

```
Match any selector    ◯    Wrap text    JavaScript         ⌄

 1   // Set up a 'click' event listener on the form element
 2 ▾ document.querySelector('form').addEventListener('click',
 3
 4       // Check the target for the "reverse-text" value
 5 ▾     if (event.target.matches('input[value="reverse-text"]
 6
 7           // If matches() returns true, toggle the 'reverse
 8           document.querySelector('body').classList.toggle('
 9       }
10
11       // Check the target for the "large-text" value
12 ▾     if (event.target.matches('input[value="large-text"]')
13
14           // If matches() returns true, toggle the 'large-te
15           document.querySelector('body').classList.toggle('

                              Cancel        Insert
```

Add a code snippet to a chat message.

To add a horizontal rule to a chat message

1. Position the insertion point in the paragraph above where you want the horizontal rule to appear in your chat message.

2. On the formatting toolbar, select **Insert horizontal rule**.

To insert a table into a chat message

1. Position the insertion point where you want the table to appear in your chat message.

2. On the formatting toolbar, select **Insert table**, and then point to the square that indicates the number of columns and rows you want in the table.

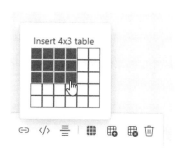

Select Insert Table and then select the size of the table you want

3. Click the square to insert the table.

4. From the formatting toolbar, you can select the **Insert column or row** command and then select one of the following commands to insert a new column or row into the table:

   - **Insert column to the right**   Inserts a new column to the right of the current column

   - **Insert column to the left**   Inserts a new column to the left of the current column

   - **Insert row above**   Inserts a new row above the current row

   - **Insert row below**   Inserts a new row below the current row

5. You can select the toolbar's **Delete column, row, or table** command and then select one of the following commands to delete data from the table:

   - **Delete column**   Deletes the current column

   - **Delete row**   Deletes the current row

   - **Delete table**   Deletes the entire table

7

Work with @mentions

One of the conveniences of chats is that no matter where you are in Teams, the app always lets you know when someone replies to a chat that you're involved in. When a reply comes in, Teams does three things:

- Teams displays a notification (and plays a sound) showing the sender's name and the first dozen or so words of the message.

- In the app bar, Teams adds a badge to the Chat button that tells you how many chats have unread messages.

- In the Chat Panel, Teams displays chats with unread messages in a bold font.

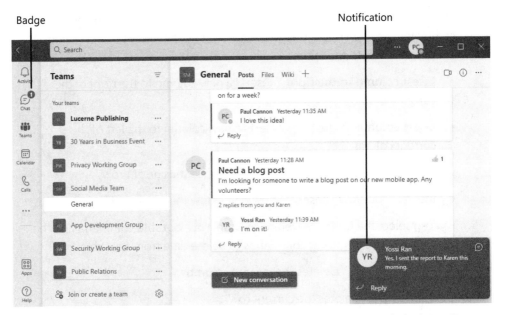

When a new message to one of your chats comes in, Teams displays a notification and a badge on the Chat button

In a group chat, however, you might want to direct a message to one person in the group. In that case, you can @mention that person. When you type @ in a chat message, Teams displays a Suggestions list that includes the chat participants, and you then select the name to complete the @mention. If this list is very long, start typing the person's name and Teams narrows the Suggestions list to just those participants whose names match your typing. When you see the person you want, select the name to complete the @mention.

Type @ to see the Suggestions list, which at first includes all the chat participants.

Now, when you post the message, only the person you @mentioned sees a notification for the message. Everyone else in the chat can see the message, but they don't receive a notification for the message (although they still see a badge on the app bar's Chat button).

 TIP To see a list of all your @mentions, type **/mentions** in the Teams **Search** box and then press **Enter** or **Return**.

To add an @mention to a chat message

1. Type @ and then start typing the name of the chat participant you want to @mention.

2. Select the person's name from the **Suggestions** list, or press **Enter** or **Return** when the name appears in the compose box.

Add a reaction to an existing chat message

Rather than replying to a chat message, you can send one of the following reactions:

- Like
- Heart (love)
- Laugh
- Surprised
- Sad
- Angry

The reaction appears in the upper-right corner of the chat message, followed by a number that indicates how many people have sent the same reaction.

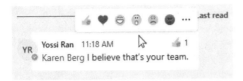

Hover the mouse over a chat message to see the available reactions.

To add a reaction to a chat message

1. Do either of the following to display the reaction lists:

    *   **Desktop or web**   Point to the chat message.

    *   **Mobile**   Long-press the chat message.

2. Select the button that represents the reaction you want to send.

Add special content to chat messages

You can spruce up your chat messages with a few special content types:

*   Emojis

*   Animated GIFs (via the Giphy service)

*   Stickers (desktop and web apps only)

*   Memes (desktop and web apps only)

As with text formatting, some caution is required here because it's easy to go overboard with this type of content, which can make your message harder to read and less likely to be taken seriously.

Teams offers several special content types that you can add to a chat message.

To add an emoji to a chat message

1. Position the insertion point where you want the emoji to appear.

2. Select the **Emoji** button.

3. Select the emoji you want to add.

To add an animated GIF to a chat message

1. Position the insertion point where you want the animated GIF to appear.

2. Do either of the following to display the animated GIFs:

   - **Desktop or web**   Select the **Giphy** button.

   - **Mobile**   Select **Add** (+) and then select **GIF**.

3. Select the animated GIF you want to add.

To add a sticker to a chat message (desktop or web app only)

1. Position the insertion point where you want the sticker to appear.

2. Select the **Sticker** button.

3. Select a category.

4. Select the sticker you want to add.

Teams offers several categories of stickers.

To add a meme to a chat message (desktop or web app only)

1. Position the insertion point where you want the meme to appear.

2. Select the **Sticker** button.

3. Select the **Meme** category.

4. Select the meme image you want to insert.

> **TIP** To upload your own meme image, select **Upload** (+), select the image in the Open dialog that appears, then select **Open**.

5. Type a top caption and a bottom caption, and then select **Done**.

Select a meme image, and then add your own captions.

Manage chat messages

To help keep your chats relevant and orderly, Teams offers quite a few chat and chat message management commands. Here are a half dozen of the most useful commands:

- **Edit**   Select this command to modify one of your chat messages. Use this command when you need to correct an error, add new text, or delete existing text.

- **Pin**   For a chat, select this command to add the chat to the Pinned section at the top of the Chat Panel. For a chat message, select this command to add the message to the top of the chat.

- **Mute**   Select this command to stop getting notifications for a chat.

- **Save this message**   Select this command to save a copy of a chat message in your Teams profile's Saved panel.

- **Share to Outlook**   Select this command to copy a chat message to an Outlook email message.

- **Delete**   Select this command to remove one of your messages from a chat.

To edit a chat message

1. Do either of the following to display the chat message management commands:

   - **Desktop or web**   Point to the chat message and then select **More options** (...).

   - **Mobile**   Long-press the chat message.

2. Select **Edit** or **Edit message** (iOS or iPadOS) to open the chat message for editing.

3. Make your changes to the chat message.

4. Select **Done** (in the desktop and web app, this is the checkmark button).

To pin a chat message (desktop and web apps only)

- Point to the chat message you want to pin, select **More options** (...), and then select **Pin**.

To pin a chat

- **Desktop or web** In the **Chat** Panel, point to the chat message, select **More options** (...) and then select **Pin**.

- **Mobile** Open a group chat message, select the chat name at the top of the screen, and then turn on the **Pin chat** switch.

To mute a chat

- In the desktop app or web app, point to the chat message, select **More options** (...), and then select **Mute**.

- In the mobile app, do any of the following:

  - Select a group chat message, select the chat name at the top of the screen, and then turn on the **Mute chat** switch.

  - In the Chat list, long-press a private chat message and then select **Mute chat**.

  - Open a private chat message, select **More options** (...). and then select **Mute chat**.

To hide a chat (desktop and web apps only)

- In the **Chat** Panel, point to the chat you want to hide, select **More options** (...), and then select **Hide**.

To save a chat message

- (Desktop or web) Point to the chat message, select **More options** (...), and then select **Save this message**.

- (Mobile) Long-press the chat message and then select **Save**.

> ⚠️ **IMPORTANT** To access your saved chat messages, select your Teams avatar and then select **Saved**. Alternatively, type /saved in the Teams **Search** box and then press **Enter** or **Return**.

To share a chat message via Outlook (desktop and web apps only)

1. Point to the chat message you want to share, select **More options** (...), and then select **Share to Outlook**.

2. Address the email message created by Teams and edit the subject line if you want to. (Teams uses the chat subject as the email subject line.)

3. Modify or introduce the chat message, if you want to.

4. Select **Send**.

To delete a chat message

- (Desktop or web) Point to the chat message, select **More options** (...), and then select **Delete**.

- (Mobile) Long-press the chat message, and then select **Delete message**.

7

Key points

- If you have several people with whom you chat regularly, be sure to either add them to your Favorites group or create a contact group for them.

- In Teams, you can create either a private chat with one other person or a group chat with two or more people.

- Although most of your chat messages will use plain text, for those times when some text formatting or some message structure such as a list would help get your message across, select the Format button to get access to all the message composition tools.

- Teams offers many tools to enhance chat messages, but don't overdo it; only use an enhancement if it adds value to your message.

- Using an @mention for a person is a useful tool for helping ensure your message is read, but you should use chat and team @mentions only rarely.

Organize meetings

You can get a lot done in Teams by using channel conversations and chats. However, there are situations, issues, and projects that require the deeper level of connection and collaboration that can only come with meeting people face-to-face. But getting everyone physically present in a meeting room these days is problematic with so many people working remotely and so many teams consisting of people who work in different cities, different states, and even different countries.

Teams helps you work around these geographical difficulties by enabling you to set up online meetings that include video and audio feeds for each participant. Meeting attendees can share content such as a window on their PC or a PowerPoint presentation, work together in breakout rooms, chat, and more.

This chapter guides you through procedures related to starting instant Teams meetings from a channel, from your Teams calendar, or from your Outlook calendar; scheduling Teams meetings from your Teams calendar, from a channel or chat, and from your Outlook calendar; and customizing meeting options before and during a Teams meeting.

In this chapter

- Start instant meetings
- Schedule meetings
- Customize meeting options

Start instant meetings

Meetings are generally prearranged affairs (see the next topic, "Schedule a meeting") because it's usually best to give the attendees some prior notice so that they can prepare for the meeting and resolve any scheduling conflicts. However, Teams also supports *instant meetings* (also called *Meet Now meetings* or *ad hoc meetings*) where you start the meeting right away and then invite people to join the meeting in progress.

Teams offers two types of instant meetings:

- **Private meeting**   This is a meeting that you start from your Teams calendar or your Outlook calendar. The meeting launches in a separate window, but it doesn't appear anywhere else in the Teams interface, so only meeting invitees can join.

- **Channel meeting**   This is a meeting that's hosted from a specific channel and is open to every member of the channel's team (assuming the channel is standard rather than private). The meeting title is usually "Meeting in *'Channel'*" (where *Channel* is the name of the channel from which the meeting was launched). The meeting itself appears in a separate window, but the channel's Posts tab also announces the meeting, shows its duration and participant avatars, offers a Join button, and displays the meeting chat. You also see a meeting-in-progress icon to the right of the channel name in the Teams panel. All files uploaded to the meeting are available in the channel's Files tab.

> ⚠ **IMPORTANT** If a team member has turned off notifications for the channel in which you're hosting a meeting, that person might not see the channel post that announces the meeting and therefore might not join the meeting. If there's a team member you want to join the meeting, be sure to invite that person after the meeting starts.

Meeting-in-progress icon   Participant avatars

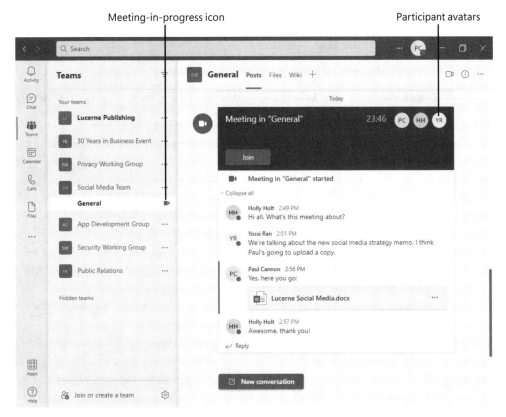

When you start a channel meeting, Teams add a new conversation topic to the channel's Posts tab.

After you start an instant meeting, you can invite other people to join. This is the only way to let potential attendees know about a private meeting. For a channel meeting, you can invite other people to join, but a Join button also appears in the channel's Posts tab while the meeting is in progress, meaning that any member of the team (assuming this is a standard channel) can join.

Teams gives you two ways to ask someone to join an in-progress instant meeting:

- **Send an invitation** The invitation appears in the form of a Teams notification that includes Accept and Decline buttons.

- **Share a meeting link** You copy a link to the meeting and then share the link via email, text message, or some other method.

To start an instant private meeting from your Teams calendar

1. In the Teams app bar, select **Calendar**.

2. To initiate the instant meeting, do one of the following:

   • **Desktop**   Select the **Meet now** button, edit the meeting name if you want to, and then select **Start meeting**.

   • **Web**   Select the **Meet now** button, edit the meeting name if you want to, and then select **Start meeting**.

   • **Mobile**   Select the **Meet now** icon.

> **TIP** (Desktop or web app only) If you want to share a link to the meeting, select **Get a link to share** and then copy the link that appears. After you start the meeting, you can paste the link into a message and send it.

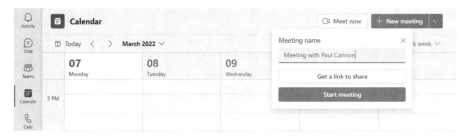

In the Teams Calendar app, select Meet Now to start an instant meeting.

3. (Desktop or web app only) Configure your audio and video settings as needed.

> 🔍 **SEE ALSO** For more information on setting up Teams audio and video for meetings, see "Manage audio and video devices" in Chapter 9, "Attend a meeting."

4. To start the instant meeting, do one of the following:

   • **Desktop**   Select **Join now**.

   • **Web**   Select **Join now**.

   • **Mobile**   Select **Start meeting**.

To start an instant private meeting from your Outlook calendar (desktop app only)

1. Display your Outlook calendar.

2. On the **Home** tab, in the **Teams Meeting** group, select **Meet now**.

3. Edit the meeting name if you want to.

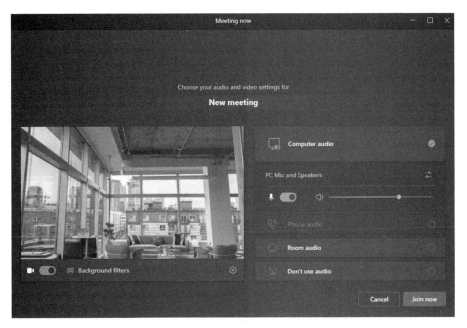

In the Outlook Calendar, select Meet Now to start an instant meeting.

4. Configure your audio and video settings as needed.

> **SEE ALSO** For more information on setting up Teams audio and video for meetings, see "Manage audio and video devices" in Chapter 9, "Attend a meeting."

5. Select **Join now** to start the instant meeting.

To start an instant channel meeting

1. In the **Posts** tab of the channel you want to meet in, do one of the following to initiate the instant meeting:

   - **Desktop** Select the **Meet now** button, edit the meeting name if you want to, and then select **Start meeting**.

- **Web**   Select the **Meet now** button, edit the meeting name if you want to, and then select **Start meeting**.

- **Mobile**   Select the **Meet now** icon.

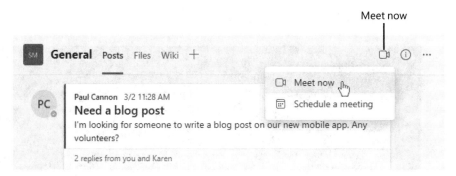

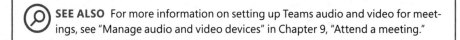

In the channel's Posts tab, select Meet Now to start an instant channel meeting.

2. Edit the meeting name, if you want to.

3. Configure your audio and video settings as needed.

> **SEE ALSO**   For more information on setting up Teams audio and video for meetings, see "Manage audio and video devices" in Chapter 9, "Attend a meeting."

4. To start the instant meeting, do one of the following:

- **Desktop**   Select **Join now**.

- **Web**   Select **Join now**.

- **Mobile**   Select **Start meeting**.

To invite people to join the meeting

1. Display the Participants pane (desktop or web) or the People screen (mobile) and then do either of the following:

- If you've just started the meeting, Teams displays the **Invite people to join you** dialog. Select **Add participants**.

- Select **Show participants**. (In the Teams smartphone app, select **More actions** (...) and then select **People**.)

2. (Mobile app only) Select **Add people**.

3. Start typing the name of the person you want to invite.

4. When the name of the person appears in the search results, send the invitation by doing one of the following:

- **Desktop**   Select the **Request to join** button that appears to the right of the person's name.

- **Web**   Select the person.

- **Mobile**   Select the person and then select **Done**.

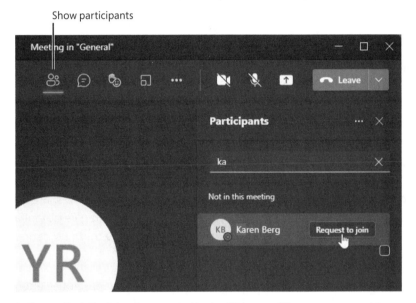

In the meeting's Participants pane, start typing the name of the person you want to invite to the meeting.

To share a meeting link

1. Do either of the following to copy the meeting link:

- If you've just started the meeting, Teams displays the **Invite people to join you** dialog. Select **Copy meeting link** (desktop or web) or **Share meeting invite** (mobile).

- Select **Show participants** to open the **Participants** pane, select **Share invite**, and then select **Copy meeting link**.

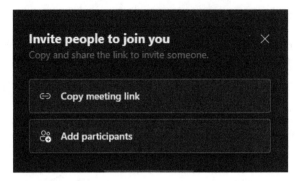

This dialog appears just after you launch your instant meeting.

2. In the desktop or web app, paste the copied link into an email, text, social media post, or some other message; in the mobile app, choose the method you want to use to share the link.

3. Send the message to the person (or people) you want to invite.

Schedule meetings

Instant meetings are useful when you just want a quick get-together to share a screen or hash out a problem. For most meetings, however, you'll want to give potential attendees plenty of notice so that everyone has time to prepare for the meeting and knows to keep the date and time free.

To give people—both team members and external users—advance notice about a meeting, you schedule the meeting. Teams enables you to set up three types of scheduled meeting:

-   **Private meeting**   This is a meeting that you schedule from your Teams calendar, from your Outlook calendar, or from a private or group chat. Only people who are invited to the meeting can join.

-   **Channel meeting**   This is a meeting that you schedule from a specific channel. For a standard channel, the meeting is open to every member of the channel's team. On the other hand, if the channel is private, then only channel members see the meeting. The meeting runs in a separate window, but the channel's Posts tab also announces the meeting, shows its duration and participant avatars, offers a Join button, and displays the meeting chat. You also see a meeting-in-progress icon to the right of the channel name in the Teams panel. Any files uploaded to the meeting are available in the channel's Files tab.

> **IMPORTANT** If a team member has turned off notifications for the channel from which you're scheduling the meeting, that member might not see the channel post that announces the meeting and therefore might not join the meeting. If there's a team member you want to join the meeting, be sure to invite that person when you schedule the meeting.

- **Webinar** This is a meeting that's open to a wider audience, which could be everyone in your organization or any member of the public who wants to attend. Attendees need to register in advance to join the webinar and can only view the webinar content that is presented. You can set up some users for direct access to the webinar and designate one or more people as presenters.

When you schedule a meeting, you provide the following details:

- **Meeting options** Select a category and specify a meeting time zone. You can also decide whether you want to request responses from the invitees and whether to allow the invitation to be forwarded. You can also set up the meeting as a webinar by requiring attendees to register for the meeting.

- **Title** Enter a name for the meeting. The title appears in the meeting invitation and in each invitee's calendar, so make the title descriptive.

- **Required attendees** Enter the names of the team members and/or the email addresses of the external users who must attend the meeting. If you create a scheduled meeting from a chat, Teams automatically adds the chat participants as required attendees.

- **Optional attendees** Enter the names of the team members and/or the email addresses of the external users whose presence at the meeting is not required for the meeting to take place.

> **TIP** You can invite anyone to a Teams meeting, even someone who doesn't have a Teams account or even the Teams desktop or mobile app. To invite an external user to a meeting, you just need to know that person's email address.

- **Date and time** Enter the date and time the meeting starts and the date and time the meeting ends. If the meeting has no set time—for example, a sales conference or team retreat—then you can schedule it as an *all-day* meeting.

Required versus optional attendees

Whatever type of meeting you schedule, you can invite one or more required attendees and/or one or more optional attendees. What's the difference between these two types of invitees? In practice, there's no difference at all! That is, both required attendees and optional attendees receive the same type of invitation. More specifically, neither invitation says anything about the person's invitation status: Required attendees aren't told their presence is a must, while optional attendees aren't told that accepting the invitation is up to them.

So, why bother differentiating between required and optional attendees? That distinction is really for you as the meeting organizer. If you define a "required" attendee as someone without whom there's no point holding the meeting, then add that person to the Required section of the meeting and keep an eye on your invitation tracking. If you see that any required person has declined the invitation, then you'll want to cancel or reschedule the meeting right away.

- **Repeat**   Enter how often you want the meeting to be scheduled:
  - Does not repeat
  - Every weekday (Mon–Fri)
  - Daily
  - Weekly
  - Monthly
  - Yearly
  - Custom (such as every two weeks or every three months)
- **Channel**   If you scheduled the meeting from your Teams calendar, your Outlook calendar, or from a chat, you can convert the private meeting to a channel meeting by specifying a channel.
- **Location**   Enter a Microsoft Teams room name, assuming your Teams administrator has set one or more rooms.

- **Details** Enter any extra information that attendees need to know about the meeting. You can format this text and add special features such as bulleted or numbered lists, tables, links, and quotations.

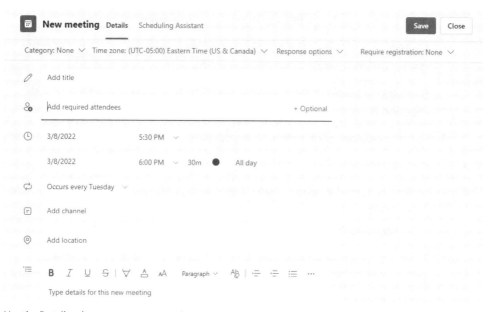

Use the Details tab to set up a new meeting

Add a calendar to a channel

The Teams calendar makes it easy to schedule a meeting because, on the meeting day, you can either just select the meeting time (to schedule a half-hour meeting at the time) or drag through the full length of the meeting duration (to schedule a meeting of that length). If you regularly create channel meetings within a particular channel, you can get these same meeting-creation conveniences by adding a calendar to that channel.

1. In the channel to which you want to add a calendar, select **Add a tab** (+).

2. In the **Add a tab** dialog, select the **Channel calendar** app, and then select **Add**.

3. In the **Channel calendar** dialog, change the tab name from the default of *Channel calendar* if you want to, and then select **Add**.

To schedule a private meeting from your Teams calendar

1. In your Teams calendar, do one of the following to tell Teams you want to schedule a meeting:

   - Select **New meeting** (desktop or web) or **New event** (+; mobile).

   - On the meeting day, select (or, in the mobile app, long-press) the meeting start time to schedule a half-hour meeting at that time.

   - (Desktop or web) On the meeting day, drag through the full length of the meeting duration to schedule a meeting of that length.

2. (Desktop or web only) Set your meeting options (**Category**, **Time zone**, and so on).

3. Type a meeting title.

4. In the **Add required attendees** box (desktop or web) or the **Add people** screen (mobile; select **Add participants** to see this screen), specify who must be at the meeting for it to proceed:

   - For a team member, start typing the person's name and then select the person when they appear in the search results.

   - For an external user, type the person's email address and then select the **Invite** *address* button (where *address* is the email address you typed).

5. (Desktop or web only) If you want to add optional attendees, select **Optional** and then specify the people whose presence at the meeting is not required:

   - For a team member, start typing the person's name and then select the person when they appear in the search results.

   - For an external user, type the person's email address and then select the **Invite** *address* button (where *address* is the email address you typed).

6. Adjust the meeting's starting and ending dates and times.

> ✅ **TIP** To help you choose a meeting time that works for all the attendees (or, at least, all the required attendees), select the **Scheduling Assistant** tab (desktop or web only). Here you see all the scheduled meetings for all your attendees, as well as some suggested meeting times if your current times contain a conflict.

7. To repeat the meeting, do one of the following:

- **Desktop or web**   Select **Does not repeat** and then select a repeat interval: **Every weekday (Mon–Fri)**, **Daily**, **Weekly**, **Monthly**, **Yearly**, or **Custom**. The **Set Recurrence** dialog appears. Specify the recurrence interval you want to use for the meeting and then select **Save**.

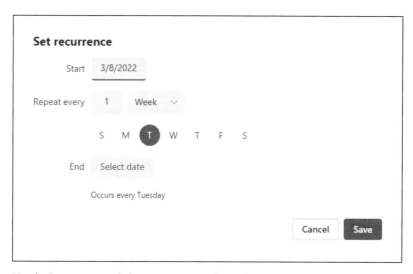

Use the Set recurrence dialog to set up a meeting series.

- **Mobile**   Select **Repeat** and then select a repeat interval: **Every day**, **Every weekday (Mon–Fri)**, **Every week**, **Every month**, or **Every year**. To specify an end time, select **Custom end time** and then select when you want the recurrence to end.

8. If your Teams admin has set up Teams rooms, use the **Add location** box (desktop or web) or the **Location** box (mobile) to choose a room.

9. Use the large compose box at the bottom of the **Details** pane to specify any other information you want to record about the meeting.

10. Select **Send** (desktop or web) or **Done** (mobile). Teams schedules the meeting and sends out the invitations to each attendee.

8

To schedule a private meeting from your Outlook calendar (desktop app only)

1. Display your Outlook calendar.

2. On the **Home** tab, select **New Teams Meeting** in the **Teams Meeting** group. Outlook displays the **Meeting** window.

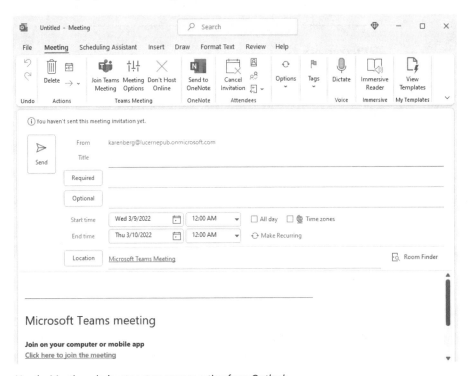

Use the Meeting window to set up your meeting from Outlook.

3. Type a meeting title.

4. Select **Required** to open the **Select Attendees and Resources** dialog and select the required attendees for your meeting:

   - For a team member, double-click the person's name in the list of contacts. Teams adds the person to the **Required** field.

   - For an external user, type the person's email address in the **Required** text box.

   - When you're done, select **OK**.

5. If you want to add optional attendees, select **Optional** and then specify the people whose presence at the meeting is not required:

   - For a team member, double-click the person's name in the list of contacts. Teams adds the person to the **Optional** field.

   - For an external user, type the person's email address in the **Optional** text box.

   - When you're done, select **OK**.

6. Adjust the meeting's starting and ending dates and times.

> ✅ **TIP** To help you choose a meeting time that works for all the attendees (or, at least, all the required attendees), select the **Scheduling Assistant** tab. Here you see all the scheduled meetings for all your attendees, as well as some suggested meeting times if your current times contain a conflict.

7. To repeat the meeting, select **Make recurring** and follow these steps in the **Appointment Recurrence** dialog that appears:

   a. Select a repeat interval: **Daily**, **Weekly**, **Monthly**, or **Yearly**.

   b. Specify the recurrence interval you want to use for the meeting.

   c. Select when you want the recurrence to end.

   d. Select **OK**.

8. If your Teams admin has set up Teams rooms, select **Location** to open the Select Rooms dialog, select a room, and then select **OK**.

9. Select **Send**. Outlook schedules the Teams meeting and sends out the invitations to each attendee.

To schedule a private meeting from a chat (desktop or web app only)

1. Select **Chat** in the app bar.

2. In the **Chat** panel, select the chat you want to use as the basis of the scheduled meeting.

8

3. Under the compose box, select **Schedule a meeting**. Teams displays the **New Meeting** screen and adds the chat participants as required attendees.

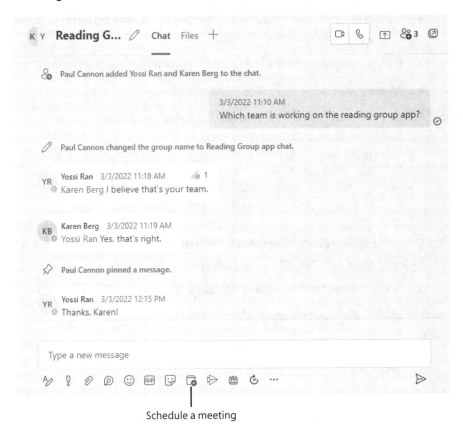

Schedule a meeting

Select the Schedule a Meeting icon to schedule a private meeting from a chat.

4. Set your meeting options (**Category**, **Time zone**, and so on).

5. Type a meeting title.

6. (Optional) Specify additional required attendees:

   - For a team member, start typing the person's name and then select the person when they appear in the search results.

   - For an external user, type the person's email address and then select the **Invite** *address* button (where *address* is the email address you typed).

7. (Optional) If you want to add optional attendees, select **Optional** and then specify the people whose presence at the meeting is not required:

    - For a team member, start typing the person's name and then select the person when they appear in the search results.

    - For an external user, type the person's email address and then select the **Invite** *address* button (where *address* is the email address you typed).

8. Adjust the meeting's starting and ending dates and times.

> ✅ **TIP** To help you choose a meeting time that works for all the attendees (or, at least, all the required attendees), select the **Scheduling Assistant** tab. Here you see all the scheduled meetings for all your attendees, as well as some suggested meeting times if your current times contain a conflict.

9. To repeat the meeting, follow these steps:

    a. Select **Does not repeat** and then select a repeat interval: **Every weekday (Mon–Fri)**, **Daily**, **Weekly**, **Monthly**, **Yearly**, or **Custom**. The **Set Recurrence** dialog appears.

    b. Specify the recurrence interval you want to use for the meeting.

    c. Select **Save**.

10. If your Teams admin has set up Teams rooms, use the **Add location** box to choose a room.

11. Use the large compose box at the bottom of the **Details** pane to specify any other information you want to record about the meeting.

12. Select **Send**. Teams schedules the meeting and sends out the invitations to each attendee.

To schedule a channel meeting (desktop or web app only)

1. Select **Teams** in the app bar.

2. Select the team you want to work with.

3. Select the channel.

8

4. Do either of the following to tell Teams you want to schedule a channel meeting:

    - In the **Posts** tab, select **Meet now** and then select **Schedule a meeting**.

    - If you added a channel calendar (see the sidebar, "Add a calendar to a channel" earlier in this topic), select the **Channel calendar** tab. On the meeting day, either select the meeting time you want (to schedule a half-hour meeting at that time) or drag through the full duration of the meeting (to schedule a meeting of that length).

5. Set your meeting options. (Note that channel meetings don't offer the **Category** option.)

6. Type a meeting title.

7. Specify required attendees:

    - For a team member, start typing the person's name and then select the person when they appear in the search results.

    - For an external user, type the person's email address and then select the **Invite** *address* button (where *address* is the email address you typed).

8. If you want to add optional attendees, select **Optional** and then specify the people whose presence at the meeting is not required:

    - For a team member, start typing the person's name and then select the person when they appear in the search results.

    - For an external user, type the person's email address and then select the **Invite** *address* button (where *address* is the email address you typed).

9. Adjust the meeting's starting and ending dates and times.

> **TIP** To help you choose a meeting time that works for all the attendees (or, at least, all the required attendees), select the **Scheduling Assistant** tab. Here, you see all the scheduled meetings for all your attendees, as well as some suggested meeting times if your current times contain a conflict.

10. To repeat the meeting, follow these steps:

    a. Select **Does not repeat** and then select a repeat interval: **Every weekday (Mon–Fri)**, **Daily**, **Weekly**, **Monthly**, **Yearly**, or **Custom**. The Set Recurrence dialog appears.

    b. Specify the recurrence interval you want to use for the meeting.

    c. Select **Save**.

11. If your Teams admin has set up Teams rooms, use the **Add location** box to choose a room.

12. Use the large compose box at the bottom of the **Details** pane to specify any other information you want to record about the meeting.

13. Select **Send**. Teams schedules the meeting and sends out the invitations to each attendee.

To schedule a webinar (desktop or web app only)

1. Display your Teams calendar.

2. Do either of the following to tell Teams you want to schedule a webinar:

   - Pull down the **New meeting** list and select **Webinar**.

   - Select **New meeting** to display the New Meeting screen, select **Require registration**, and then select **For everyone**.

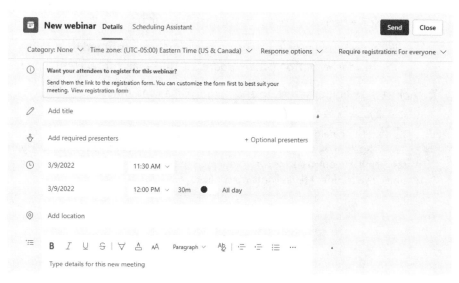

Use the New Webinar screen to set up your webinar.

8

3. Set your webinar options (**Category**, **Time zone**, and so on).

> **TIP** If you want to restrict your webinar registrants to just people in your organization, select **Require registration** and then select **For people in your org**.

> **TIP** By default, when people register for your webinar, the form they see asks for each person's first name, last name, and email address. To customize this form, select the **View registration form** link, and then select **Add field** in the window that appears. Select a field such as **Industry** or **Job title**. You can also select **Custom question** to ask for custom information from each attendee.

4. Type a webinar title.

5. In the **Add required presenters** box, specify who must present content at the webinar:

    - For a team member, start typing the person's name and then select the person when they appear in the search results.

    - For an external user, type the person's email address and then select the **Invite** *address* button (where *address* is the email address you typed).

6. If you want to add optional presenters, select **Optional** and then specify the people who can optionally present content at the webinar:

    - For a team member, start typing the person's name and then select the person when they appear in the search results.

    - For an external user, type the person's email address and then select the **Invite** *address* button (where *address* is the email address you typed).

7. Adjust the webinar's starting and ending dates and times.

> **TIP** To help you choose a webinar time that works for all the presenters (or, at least, all the required presenters), select the **Scheduling Assistant** tab. Here, you see all the scheduled events for all your presenters, as well as some suggested webinar times if your current times contain a conflict.

8. If your Teams admin has set up Teams rooms, use the **Add location** box to choose a room.

9. Use the large compose box at the bottom of the **Details** pane to specify any other information you want to record about the webinar.

10. Select **Send**. Teams schedules the webinar and sends out the invitations to each presenter.

> **TIP** To get the webinar's registration link to share with the public or with people in your organization, select **Calendar** in the Teams app bar, select the webinar, and then select **Edit**. In the **Details** tab, select **Copy registration link**. You can now paste the link using whatever media you want to use to let people know about your webinar.

To track a scheduled meeting's invitations

1. In your Teams calendar, select the meeting you want to track.

2. (Desktop or web only) Select **Edit**.

3. If you set up the meeting with a recurrence interval, select either **Edit occurrence** (to edit just the meeting you selected) or **Edit series** (to edit all the meetings in the recurrence series).

4. Examine the responses in the **Tracking** pane (desktop or web) or the **Participants** sections of the **Details** pane (mobile).

To cancel a scheduled, non-repeating meeting

1. In your Teams calendar, select the meeting you want to cancel.

2. (Desktop or web only) Select **Edit**.

3. To cancel the meeting, do one of the following:

   - **Desktop** Select **Cancel meeting**, type an optional cancellation note, and then select **Cancel meeting**.

   - **Web** Select **Cancel meeting**, type an optional cancellation note, and then select **Cancel meeting**.

   - **Mobile** Select **Cancel event**, and then select **Cancel event** (Android or iOS) or **Confirm** (iPadOS).

8

To cancel one occurrence of a scheduled, repeating meeting

1. In your Teams calendar, select the meeting occurrence you want to cancel.

2. (Desktop or web only) Select **Edit** and then select **Edit occurrence**.

3. To cancel the occurrence, do one of the following:

   - **Desktop** Select **Cancel meeting**, select **Cancel occurrence**, type an optional cancellation note, then select **Cancel occurrence**.

   - **Web** Select **Cancel meeting**, select **Cancel occurrence**, type an optional cancellation note, then select **Cancel occurrence**.

   - **Mobile** Select **Cancel occurrence** and then select **Cancel occurrence** (Android or iOS) or **Confirm** (iPadOS).

To cancel all occurrences of a scheduled, repeating meeting

1. In your Teams calendar, select any meeting in the series you want to cancel.

2. (Desktop or web only) Select **Edit** and then select **Edit series**.

3. To cancel the series, do one of the following:

   - **Desktop** Select **Cancel meeting**, select **Cancel series**, type an optional cancellation note, and then select **Cancel series**.

   - **Web** Select **Cancel meeting**, select **Cancel series**, type an optional cancellation note, and then select **Cancel series**.

   - **Mobile** Select **View series**, select **Cancel series**, and then select **Cancel series** (Android or iOS) or **Confirm** (iPadOS).

To start a scheduled meeting

1. In your Teams calendar, select the scheduled meeting.

2. Select **Join**.

3. Configure your audio and video settings as needed.

 **SEE ALSO** For more information on setting up Teams audio and video for meetings, see "Manage audio and video devices" in Chapter 9, "Attend meetings."

4. Select **Join now**.

Customize meeting options

The default settings that Teams applies to instant meetings, scheduled meetings, and webinars are fine for most people's needs. However, you might come across situations where you need to use some custom settings. For example, you might create a meeting where you only want to present content to the attendees, so in that case, it would be best to customize the meeting to prevent each attendee from turning on their microphone and camera. Similarly, for a particularly important meeting, you might want to disable potential distractions such as chat and reactions.

For these and similar situations, Teams offers the following meeting options for the meeting organizer:

- **Who can bypass the lobby?** Choose who is allowed directly into the meeting instead of having to wait in the meeting's lobby for the organizer to allow access.

- **Always let callers bypass the lobby** Toggle this switch to **Yes** to give dial-in users direct access to the meeting instead of waiting in the lobby to be admitted.

- **Announce when callers join or leave** Toggle this switch to **No** to disable Teams making an announcement each time a dial-in user joins or leaves the meeting.

- **Who can present?** Choose who can share content in the meeting. The default for regular meetings is **Everyone**, while the default for webinars is **Specific people**. If you choose **Specific people**, Teams adds the **Choose presenters** option, which enables you to specify who can present during the meeting.

- **Allow mic for attendees?** Toggle this switch to **No** to disable the microphone for the meeting attendees. Disabling microphones is useful for meetings that only present content (such as a webinar, where this setting is **No** by default).

- **Allow camera for attendees?** Toggle this switch to **No** to disable the camera for meeting attendees. Again, disabling cameras is useful for meetings that only present content (such as a webinar, where this setting is **No** by default).

- **Record automatically** Toggle this switch to **Yes** to have Teams start a recording of the meeting automatically as soon as you start the meeting.

 SEE ALSO For more information on recording meetings, see "Record a meeting" in Chapter 10, "Get things done in a meeting."

8

- **Allow meeting chat**   Select **Enabled** or **Disabled** to allow or disallow, respectively, meeting participants to chat. If you want to allow participants to chat only when the meeting is taking place, select **In-meeting only**.

- **Allow reactions**   Toggle this switch to **No** to disable reactions in the meeting.

- **Provide CART captions**   Toggle this switch to **Yes** to provide the communication access real-time (CART) service during your meeting, where a trained CART captioner translates all meeting speech into captions. If you enable this option, when you select **Save**, Teams generates a URL. Select **Copy link** and then send the URL to your CART captioner.

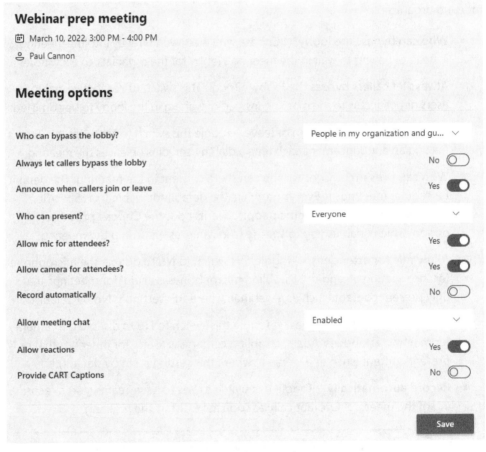

Webinar prep meeting

📅 March 10, 2022, 3:00 PM - 4:00 PM

👤 Paul Cannon

Meeting options

Who can bypass the lobby?	People in my organization and gu... ⌄
Always let callers bypass the lobby	No ⦸
Announce when callers join or leave	Yes ⬤
Who can present?	Everyone ⌄
Allow mic for attendees?	Yes ⬤
Allow camera for attendees?	Yes ⬤
Record automatically	No ⦸
Allow meeting chat	Enabled ⌄
Allow reactions	Yes ⬤
Provide CART Captions	No ⦸

Save

Use the Meeting Options web page to modify your meeting's settings.

You can set these options prior to a scheduled meeting or webinar, or you can adjust these options while your meeting is in progress.

To set meeting options for a scheduled meeting

1. In your Teams calendar, select the meeting.

2. (Desktop or web only) Select **Edit**.

3. In the **Details** tab, select the **Meeting options** button.

4. On the Meeting Options page, modify the meeting options as needed, and then select **Save**.

To set meeting options during a meeting (desktop app only)

1. On the meeting toolbar, select **More actions (...)**, and then select **Meeting options**.

While a meeting is in progress, use the Meeting Options pane to modify your meeting's settings.

2. In the **Meeting options** pane, modify the meeting options as needed.

3. Select **Save**.

Key points

- Create an instant meeting if you want to run a quick meeting with a few people to share a document or resolve a problem.

- Schedule a meeting when you want to give attendees enough time to prepare for the meeting and to reserve a block of time for people to attend.

- Organize a channel meeting when the meeting topic is channel-specific and you want to allow any channel member to attend without having to send out invitations.

- Set up a webinar when you want to present content to your organization or to the general public.

- Required attendees are people without whom there's no point or need to hold the meeting.

- The quickest way to create an instant private meeting is to open your Teams calendar and select the Meet now button.

- To create an instant channel meeting, select the channel and then select the Meet now button in the Posts tab.

- The quickest way to schedule a private meeting is to open your Teams calendar and then either select the meeting start time (to schedule a half-hour meeting at that time) or drag through the full length of the meeting duration (to schedule a meeting of that length).

Attend meetings

Teams meetings have essentially three steps: organizing, attending, and participating. Getting meetings set up and off the ground was the subject of Chapter 8, "Organize meetings." Participating in a meeting is the subject of Chapter 10, "Get things done in meetings." Between the organizing and the participating, however, is the attending, which here means joining an instant or scheduled meeting, getting your camera and microphone set up the way you want, and customizing the meeting to suit your preferences.

This chapter guides you through procedures related to responding to meeting invitations, joining meetings, managing audio and video devices, customizing your meeting settings while attending meetings, and managing meeting attendees.

In this chapter

- Respond to meeting invitations
- Join meetings
- Manage audio and video devices
- Customize your meeting settings
- Manage meeting attendees

Respond to meeting invitations

When the meeting organizer sends you an invitation to join an instant or scheduled meeting, you must send a response so the organizer knows whether you're attending. Depending on the type of meeting and how you elect to respond to the invitation, you have as many as four ways to respond:

- **Accept**   Return this response if you'll be attending the meeting.

- **Decline**   Return this response if you won't be attending the meeting.

- **Tentative**   Return this response if you're not sure whether you can attend the meeting.

- **Propose New Time**   Return this response if the meeting time doesn't work for you, and you want to suggest a different time.

To respond to a meeting invitation

- If you receive a Teams invitation to an instant meeting, select **Accept** or **Decline**.

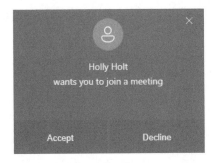

A notification for an instant meeting

- If you receive an email invitation to a scheduled meeting, select **Accept** or **Decline**. You can also select **Tentative** if you're not certain you can attend. If the meeting time doesn't work for you, you can select **Propose New Time**, select either **Tentative and Propose New Time** or **Decline and Propose New Time**, select a time that works for you, and then select **Propose Time**.

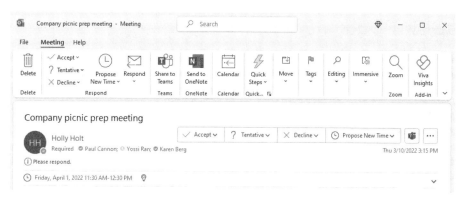

An email invitation for a scheduled meeting

■ After you receive an invitation for a scheduled meeting, a temporary event for the meeting appears in your Teams calendar. Select **Calendar** in the Teams app bar, select the meeting, select **RSVP**, and then select **Accept**, **Tentative**, or **Decline**. If the meeting repeats, select **RSVP**, select either **Respond to occurrence** or **Respond to series**, and then select your response.

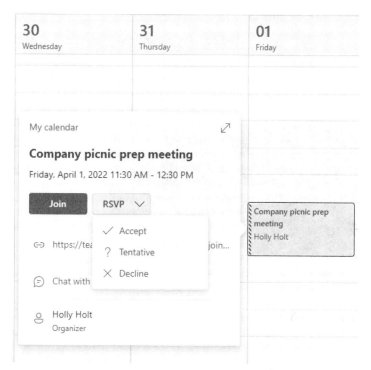

For a scheduled meeting, select the temporary event in the Teams calendar and then select RSVP to respond.

Join meetings

If a meeting you want to attend is already in progress, or if the start time of a scheduled meeting that you've been invited to has arrived, then your next step is to join the meeting. Whatever type of meeting you join, Teams first displays a window where you can choose the microphone and camera you want to use for the meeting, whether these devices are turned off when you join, and a few other audio and video settings.

How you join a meeting depends on the type of meeting and how the meeting organizer invited you. There are five main possibilities for joining a meeting:

- Join an instant meeting via your Activity feed if you missed the meeting notification.
- Join via your Teams calendar.
- Join via your Outlook calendar.
- Join a channel meeting via the channel's Posts tab.
- Join by selecting an email invitation link or meeting link.

Most of the time, particularly if you're in the same organization as the person who set up the meeting, joining the meeting means you get into the meeting straight away. However, it's possible the meeting organizer has restricted who get direct access to the meeting, which means everyone else must wait in the meeting's lobby to gain access.

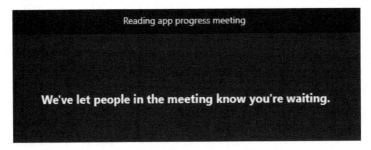

The message you see when you're in the meeting lobby waiting to be let in by a meeting organizer

To join a meeting from your Activity feed

1. In the Teams app bar, select **Activity** to display the Feed panel.
2. Select the meeting notification.

3. Select **Join**.

4. Set up your preferred video and audio devices and settings.

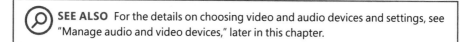

SEE ALSO For the details on choosing video and audio devices and settings, see "Manage audio and video devices," later in this chapter.

5. Select **Join now**. Teams either lets you into the meeting or places you in the meeting lobby, where you must wait until a meeting organizer lets you into the meeting.

To join a meeting from your Teams calendar

1. In the Teams app bar, select **Calendar**.

2. Navigate to the day on which the meeting occurs.

3. Select the meeting's **Join** button. (You can also select the meeting and then select **Join**.) Teams displays the **Choose Your Video and Audio Options** window.

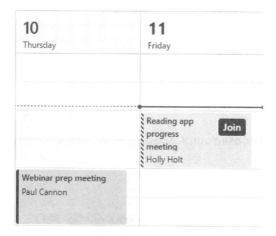

In your Teams calendar, select the meeting's Join button.

4. Set up your preferred video and audio devices and settings.

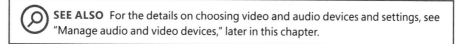

SEE ALSO For the details on choosing video and audio devices and settings, see "Manage audio and video devices," later in this chapter.

5. Select **Join now**. Teams either lets you into the meeting or places you in the meeting lobby where you must wait until a meeting organizer lets you into the meeting.

To join a meeting from your Outlook calendar (desktop app only)

1. In Outlook, select **Calendar**.

2. Navigate to the day on which the meeting occurs.

3. Select the meeting.

4. In the **Meeting** tab, select **Join Teams Meeting**. Teams displays the **Choose Your Video and Audio Options** window.

5. Set up your preferred video and audio devices and settings.

> (🔍) **SEE ALSO** For the details on choosing video and audio devices and settings, see "Manage audio and video devices," later in this chapter.

6. Select **Join now**. Teams either lets you into the meeting or places you in the meeting lobby, where you must wait until a meeting organizer lets you into the meeting.

To join a channel meeting

1. In the Teams app bar, select **Teams**.

2. Select the team.

3. Select the channel.

4. In the **Posts** tab, select the **Join** button in the post that announces the channel meeting. Teams displays the **Choose Your Video and Audio Options** window.

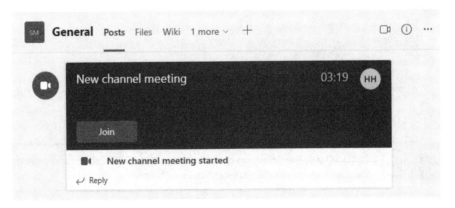

In the channel's Teams calendar, select the meeting's Join button.

5. Set up your preferred video and audio devices and settings.

 SEE ALSO For the details on choosing video and audio devices and settings, see "Manage audio and video devices," later in this chapter.

6. Select **Join now**. Teams either lets you into the meeting or places you in the meeting lobby, where you must wait until a meeting organizer lets you into the meeting.

To join a meeting from an email invitation or link

1. Open the meeting invitation or the message that contains the link.

2. For an email invitation, select the **Click here to join the meeting** link; otherwise, select the meeting link. Your default web browser opens and lets you know that teams.microsoft.com is trying to open Microsoft Teams.

⚠ **IMPORTANT** The notification you see depends on which web browser you're using. The notification shown in the figure and handled in Steps 3 and 4 are from Microsoft Edge.

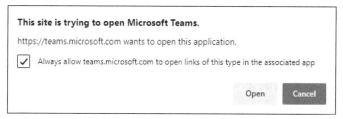

When you click the link to join a meeting, your web browser asks for permission to open Teams.

3. Select the checkbox that allows the Teams website to open meeting links. Selecting this checkbox means that, in the future, when you click a meeting link, you can skip Steps 3 and 4.

4. Select **Open**.

5. Teams displays the **Choose Your Video and Audio Options** window.

9

6. Set up your preferred video and audio devices and settings.

> **SEE ALSO** For the details on choosing video and audio devices and settings, see "Manage audio and video devices," later in this chapter.

7. Select **Join now**. Teams either lets you into the meeting or places you in the meeting lobby where you must wait until a meeting organizer lets you into the meeting.

Manage audio and video devices

For most Teams meetings, you need three devices:

- A video camera so that meeting attendees can see you

- A microphone so that meeting attendees can hear you

- A speaker so that you can hear what the other meeting attendees have to say

There are some exceptions where you don't need all three devices. For example, many people use a headset that combines a microphone and a speaker. Similarly, if you join a webinar as a viewer, you won't need a video camera or microphone because webinars are meant to be one-way, presentation-only meetings.

Teams gives you two opportunities to choose and configure your audio and video devices for a particular meeting: Just before you join a meeting and while you're participating in a meeting.

Just prior to joining a meeting, the Teams desktop app displays the Choose Your Video and Audio Options window. This window offers video-related options on the left and audio-related options on the right. For your video devices, you see the following features on the left side of the window:

- **Video feed** The bulk of the left side of the window is taken up by a live video feed from your video camera.

- **Camera** This switch toggles the video camera on and off. If you prefer to start the meeting with no video feed, set this switch to Off.

- **Background filters**   Select this command to display the Background Settings pane, which enables you to apply a custom background to your video feed.

> **SEE ALSO**   To learn more about applying a background filter, see "Customize your meeting settings," later in this chapter.

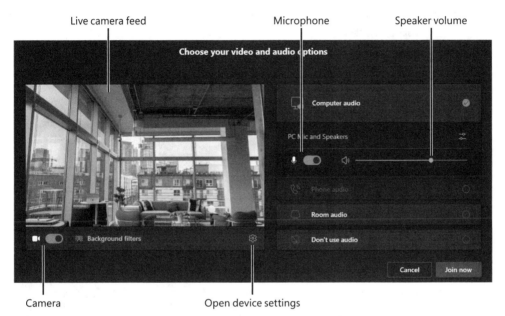

Just before you join a meeting, Teams gives you a chance to choose and configure your audio and video devices.

For your audio devices, the right side of the window consists mostly of four audio device choices:

- **Computer audio**   Select this option to use the default microphone and speaker that are connected to your computer. There are two controls associated with the Computer audio option:
  - **Microphone**   This switch toggles the microphone on and off. If you prefer to start the meeting with your microphone muted, set this switch to Off.
  - **Speaker volume**   Use this slider to set the volume of your speakers.
- **Phone audio**   Select this option to participate in the audio portion of the meeting using your phone. After you join the meeting, you can connect the audio portion either by having the meeting dial your phone number or by

dialing in to the meeting yourself from a list of numbers. You need an audio conferencing license to use the phone audio method.

- **Room audio**   Select this option to use the audio devices associated with a particular Teams room. After you select this option, use the Search for a room combo box to find the room that has the devices you want to use.

- **Don't use audio**   Select this option to join the meeting with your microphone and speakers muted.

For more audio and video device options, including choosing a different computer microphone and/or speakers, select Open device settings to display the Device settings pane. The Audio Settings section of this pane includes the following options:

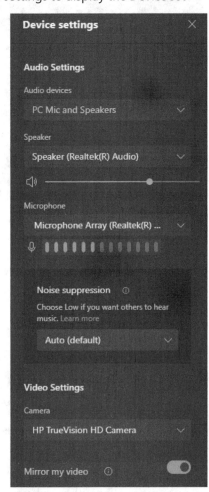

- **Audio devices**   Use this list to select the combined (microphone and speaker) device you want to use.

- **Speaker**   Use this list to select the speaker you want to use. Use the slider under this list to set the speaker volume.

- **Microphone**   Use this list to select the microphone you want to use. Speak into the microphone, and then use the meter under this list to check your microphone volume level.

- **Noise suppression**   Use this list to select the level of noise suppression you want to use. Noise suppression is a technique that reduces the amount of background noise picked up by your microphone. Auto is usually the best choice because it lets Teams determine how much suppression is needed. If attendees complain about background noises in your feed, choose High instead. If you're playing music or other sounds that you want attendees to hear, choose Low or even Off instead.

Select Open Device Settings to display the Device Settings pane.

The Video Settings section of the Device Settings pane includes the following options:

- **Camera**   Use this list to select the video camera you want to use.

- **Mirror my video**   When this switch is on, when you look at your video feed during the meeting, the feed will appear the same as if you were looking in a mirror. If you find this disorienting, especially if you hold up signs or other text that appear backward, set the Mirror my video switch to Off.

 IMPORTANT   The Mirror My Video switch has no effect on how meeting attendees see your video feed; it only affects how you see your own feed.

All of the above settings apply to the Teams desktop app, and the Teams web app offers a similar set of options (minus the choice of audio devices). The settings for the mobile app are much simpler:

- **Camera**   This switch toggles the mobile device video camera on and off. If you prefer to start the meeting with no video feed, set this switch to Off.

- **Microphone**   This switch toggles the mobile device microphone on and off. If you prefer to start the meeting with no audio feed, set this switch to Off.

- **Audio**   This menu enables you to choose your mobile audio device. If you want to start the meeting with both incoming and outgoing audio turned off, select Audio off.

- **Background effects**   Select this command to display the Select Background screen, which enables you to apply a custom background to your video feed.

Use this screen to configure your mobile audio and video devices before joining a meeting.

 SEE ALSO   To learn more about applying a background effect, see "Customize your meeting settings," later in this chapter.

To select your meeting devices and settings

- **Before joining a meeting** In the **Choose your video and audio options** window, select your devices and settings.

- **After joining a meeting** Do one of the following:

    - **Desktop** On the meeting toolbar, select **More actions (...)**, select **Device settings**, and then in the **Device Settings** pane, select your devices and settings.

    - **Web** On the meeting toolbar, select **More actions (...)**, select **Show device settings** (web), and then in the Device Settings pane, select your devices and settings.

 TIP This option is not available in the Teams mobile app.

To mute or unmute your audio

- On the meeting toolbar, select **Mute** or **Unmute**.

- Press **Ctrl+Shift+M**.

Select Mute to turn off your audio feed.

To turn on your audio devices

- **Desktop** On the meeting toolbar, select **Turn audio on**. In the **Turn audio on?** dialog, select **Turn audio on**.

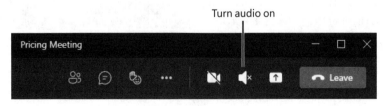

Select Turn Audio On to turn on your microphone and speaker.

■ **Mobile**   On the meeting toolbar, select (Android) or long-press (iOS or iPadOS) the **Audio** button and then select the mobile audio device option you want to use.

 TIP This option is not available in the Teams web app.

To turn off your video

■ On the meeting toolbar, select **Camera**.

To turn on your video

■ On the meeting toolbar, select **Camera**.

■ (Desktop only) On the meeting toolbar, point to the **Camera** button to display the Private Preview window. If you want to, choose a different camera or apply a background effect. When you're ready to turn on your video feed, select **Camera** in the meeting toolbar.

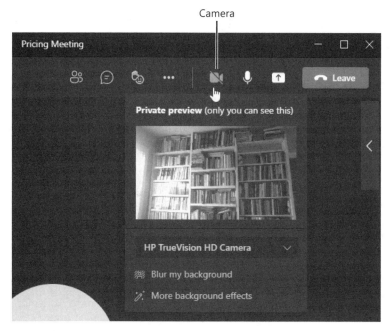

Point to the Camera button to see more camera options.

9

Customize your meeting settings

When you first enter a meeting, you'll likely have a bit of time before the meeting gets going to customize certain settings to suit the way you work and how you want the meeting to look. However, the customization settings are available throughout the meeting, so feel free to make changes whenever you think they're needed.

> ⚠️ **IMPORTANT** Although you can make changes at any time during the meeting, there's one setting you should consider making at the beginning of the meeting: your background effect. Depending on the effect, changing the background of your video feed can be jarring and distracting, so getting this customization out of the way early (ideally, before you join the meeting) is best.

One of the most common meeting customizations is the application of a background effect, which either alters your current video background or replaces that background with a different image. Using the Background Settings pane, there are three types of background effects you can apply:

- **Blur** This effect keeps your current video background but blurs it so that meeting participants can't see any details.

- **Predefined image** This effect replaces your video background with an image supplied by Teams. There are more than two dozen images that include office and home interiors, landscapes, shapes, and gaming and science fiction scenes.

- **Custom image** This effect replaces your video background with an image supplied by you.

> ⚠️ **IMPORTANT** The custom image must be in one of the following file formats: JPEG, PNG, or BMP. Also, the image file must be no smaller than 360 x 360 px but no larger than 2048 x 2048 px. Finally, the file's aspect ratio (the ratio of its width to its height) must be greater than 4:3 (such as 3:2 or 16:9, but nòt 1:1 or 5:4).

> ⚠️ **IMPORTANT** Background effects can be fun, and they can enhance privacy by hiding your actual background. However, be aware that some backgrounds are very distracting.

You can customize your video background with a blur effect, a predefined background image, or a custom image.

9

Teams also offers several options for customizing the meeting view. Most of the options affect the *gallery*, which is the collection of participant video feeds (or static avatars or initials for those participants who've turned off their video). Here are the options:

- **Large gallery (available in all versions of the Teams app)**   Select this command in a large meeting to display up to 49 participant video feeds at a time, with navigation controls that enable you to see more pages of video feeds.

- **Together mode (desktop and web apps only)**   Select this command to display participants' faces close to each other using a virtual background such as an auditorium, amphitheater, or conference room.

- **Gallery on top (desktop only)**   Select this command to display the gallery of participants above the content that is being shared.

A Teams meeting with the gallery on top

- **Focus on content (desktop only)**   Select this command to hide the gallery and see only the content that a participant is sharing.

- **Full screen (desktop only)**   Select this command to hide the meeting window title bar and give the meeting content the full height and width of the screen.

- **Turn on live captions (desktop and mobile apps only)**   Select this command to enable *live captions*, which is a Teams feature that transcribes what's being said in the meeting and presents it in real-time as captions that appear at the bottom of the meeting window.

Teams also gives you some control over what gets shown in the meeting window, mostly so you can turn off some features to avoid distractions. Teams enables you to turn off the following features:

- **Incoming video (available in all versions of the Teams app)**   This prevents you from seeing the video feeds for all the meeting participants.

- **Chat bubbles (desktop only)** This prevents you from seeing the pop-up messages that appear onscreen when someone posts a message to the meeting chat.

- **Meeting notifications (desktop only)** This prevents you from seeing all meeting notifications (for example, when a dial-up attendee joins or leaves).

To apply a background effect to your video (desktop and mobile apps only)

1. On the meeting toolbar, select **More actions** (...).

2. Do one of the following:

   - **Desktop** Select **Apply background effect** to display the Background Settings pane. If you want to see what the effect will look like before applying it, select **Preview**.

   - **Mobile** Select **Background effect** to display the Select Background screen.

3. Select the effect you want:

   - To blur your video background, select **Blur**.

   - To replace your video background with a predefined image, select the image.

   - To replace your video background with a custom image, select **Add new** (desktop) or **+** (mobile), select the image file you want to use, and then select **Open** (desktop).

4. Apply the new background effect:

   - **Desktop** Select **Apply**. If you currently have your video turned off, select **Apply and turn on video** instead.

   - **Mobile** Select **Done**. If you currently have your video turned off, select **Yes** when Teams asks if you want to turn on your camera.

To change your view of the meeting attendees (desktop app)

- On the meeting toolbar, select **More actions** (...), and then select the command that represents the view you want to use (such as **Together mode** or **Large gallery**).

To change your view of the meeting attendees (Android app)

- On the meeting toolbar, select **More actions** (...), select **Meeting views**, and then select the command that represents the view you want to use.

9

To change your view of the meeting attendees (iOS app)

■ On the meeting toolbar, select **More actions** (...), select **Views**, and then select the command that represents the view you want to use.

To turn on live captions (desktop and mobile apps only)

■ On the meeting toolbar, select **More actions** (...), and then select **Turn on live captions**.

To disable or enable incoming video

■ On the meeting toolbar, select **More actions** (...), and then select **Turn off incoming video** or **Turn on incoming video**.

To disable or enable chat bubbles (desktop app only)

■ On the meeting toolbar, select **More actions** (...), and then select **Don't show chat bubbles** or **Show chat bubbles**.

To disable or enable meeting notifications (desktop app only)

■ On the meeting toolbar, select **More actions** (...), and then select **Mute notifications** or **Allow notifications**.

Manage meeting attendees

Teams gives you quite a bit of control over how other meeting attendees appear in the meeting, not only just to you, but in some cases, to everyone else in the meeting.

If you're the meeting organizer, one meeting option you might have set up is to have some or all attendees wait in the lobby for you to let them in to the meeting. This is a useful security feature because it enables you to deny entrance to anyone you don't recognize. The Participants pane maintains a Waiting in lobby section that tells you who's waiting to be let in. From there, you can admit or deny, as needed.

 SEE ALSO To learn how to set up a meeting to have some or all participants wait in the lobby, see "Customize meeting options" in Chapter 8, "Organize meetings."

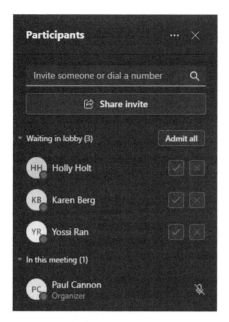

The meeting lobby

While you're in the meeting, Teams also lets you perform the following attendee-related chores:

- **Add an attendee** You can invite more people to the meeting as needed.

- **Pin an attendee** When you *pin* an attendee, it means that person's video feed always takes up the bulk of the meeting window, no matter whether that person is talking or not. (In a normal meeting, the bulk of the meeting window is taken up by whoever is currently talking.)

- **Hide your video feed** If you don't want to see your own video feed in the gallery, you can hide it. Teams displays your video as a stub in the bottom-right corner (or the top-right corner, if you have the Gallery at top command enabled) of the screen. Select that stub to unhide your video.

9

Teams displays your hidden video feed as a stub, usually in the bottom-right corner of the meeting window.

- **Spotlight an attendee** When you *spotlight* an attendee, it means that person's video feed always takes up the bulk of the meeting window for every meeting participant, no matter whether that person is talking or not. (In a normal meeting, the bulk of the meeting window is taken up by whoever is currently talking.)

- **Mute an attendee** You can turn off a meeting participant's audio feed. This is useful if that person's audio is causing a distraction.

- **Remove an attendee** You can force a participant to leave the meeting if that person is being disruptive.

To let in attendees who are waiting in the lobby

1. Do either of the following to view the meeting lobby:

   - On the meeting toolbar, select **Show Participants** to open the Participants pane.

   - If the notification that one or more people are waiting in the lobby is onscreen, select **View Lobby**.

Teams displays this notification when one or more people are waiting in the meeting lobby.

2. In the **Waiting in lobby** section, select **Allow** (the green checkmark) to let in a waiting attendee. If you don't recognize the person, you can remove that person from the lobby and prevent them from joining your meeting by selecting **Decline** (the red X) instead.

3. Repeat Step 2 for each person waiting in the lobby.

> 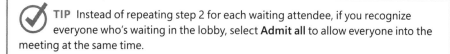 **TIP** Instead of repeating step 2 for each waiting attendee, if you recognize everyone who's waiting in the lobby, select **Admit all** to allow everyone into the meeting at the same time.

To add an attendee to an in-progress meeting

1. Select **Show participants**. (In the Teams smartphone app, select **More actions (...)** and then select **People**.)

2. (Mobile app only) Select **Add people**.

3. Start typing the name of the person you want to invite.

4. When the name of the person appears in the search results, do one of the following to send the invitation:

- **Desktop**   Select the **Request to join** button that appears to the right of the person's name.

- **Web**   Select the person.

- **Mobile**   Select the person and then select **Done**.

To pin an attendee to the top of the Participants pane

- **Desktop, web, and tablet**   On the meeting toolbar, select **Show Participants** to open the Participants pane, select the attendee's **More options (...)** button, and then select **Pin for me**.

- **Mobile**   Select **More actions (...)**, select **People** to open the Meeting Participants pane, select the attendee, and then select **Pin for me**.

To hide your own video feed (desktop app only)

- On the meeting toolbar, select **Show Participants** to open the Participants pane, select your **More options (...)** button, and then select **Hide for me**.

- In the meeting gallery, select your **More options (...)** button and then select **Hide for me**.

To spotlight an attendee's video

- **Desktop**   On the meeting toolbar, select **Show Participants** to open the Participants pane, select the attendee's **More options (...)** button, and then select **Spotlight for everyone**. When Teams asks you to confirm, select **Spotlight for everyone**.

- **Mobile (tablet)**   On the meeting toolbar, select **Show Participants**. In the **Meeting Participants** pane, select the attendee, and then select **Spotlight for everyone**. When Teams asks you to confirm, select **Spotlight**.

- **Mobile**

  - (Smartphone)   Select **More actions (...)**, select **People** to open the Meeting Participants pane, select the attendee, and then select **Spotlight for everyone**. When Teams asks you to confirm, select **Spotlight**.

  - (Desktop only) In the meeting gallery, select the attendee's **More options (...)** button and then select **Spotlight for everyone**. When Teams asks you to confirm, select **Spotlight for everyone**.

TIP This feature is not available in the Teams web app.

To mute an attendee (desktop and web apps only)

- On the meeting toolbar, select **Show Participants** to open the Participants pane, select the attendee's **More options (...)** button, and then select **Mute participant**.

- In the meeting gallery, select the attendee's **More options (...)** button and then select **Mute participant**.

To mute all attendees (desktop app only)

1. On the meeting toolbar, select **Show Participants**.

2. In the **Participants** pane, select **Mute all**.

3. In the **Mute everyone?** dialog, select **Mute**.

Teams displays this confirmation when you select the Mute All button.

To remove an attendee

- **Desktop**   On the meeting toolbar, select **Show Participants**. In the **Participants** pane, select the attendee's **More options (...)** button, and then select **Remove from meeting**.

- **Web**   On the meeting toolbar, select **Show Participants**. In the **People** pane, select the attendee's **More options (...)** button, and then select **Remove from meeting**.

- **Mobile (tablet)**   On the meeting toolbar, select **Show Participants**. In the **Meeting Participants** pane, select the attendee, and then select **Remove from meeting**.

- **Mobile (smartphone)**   On the meeting toolbar, select **More actions (...)**, and then select **People**. In the **Meeting Participants** pane, select the attendee, and then select **Remove from meeting**.

Key points

- You usually respond to a meeting invitation by either accepting or declining the invitation. You can also respond that you're tentative if you're not sure you can attend, or you can propose a new time.

- When you select a meeting invitation link and your web browser asks for permission to open the Microsoft Teams app, before you select the Open button, be sure to select the checkbox to always allow the browser to open meeting links in the Teams app.

- When you join a meeting, you might have to wait in the lobby for the meeting organizer to let you in.

- Before you join a meeting, be sure to choose the audio and video devices you prefer to use.

- You should usually join a meeting with your microphone either muted or disabled.

- Using a video background effect is useful if you don't want others to see your actual background, but choose your background carefully and avoid images that are too busy or distracting.

Get things done in meetings

The scourge of the modern workplace is the too-long meeting that produces too little in the way of solutions or resolutions. That outcome can happen with both in-person meetings and with Teams virtual meetings. However, it seems to happen less often with virtual meetings because Teams gives each participant a variety of tools to interact, share, and collaborate. The secret to getting things done in a Teams meeting is to not only get to know these tools but also to learn how to use them judiciously.

This chapter guides you through procedures related to recording a meeting and interacting with other meeting attendees by raising your hand, sending reactions, and chatting. You also learn how to share content, such as a screen, window, whiteboard, and file, how to share information using your device camera, and how to present a PowerPoint slideshow. This chapter shows you how to work with breakout rooms, including how to create them, assign them to attendees, open them, and join them. Finally, this chapter also shows you how to leave and end a meeting.

In this chapter

- Record meetings
- Interact in meetings
- Present content in meetings
- Manage breakout rooms
- Close a meeting

Record meetings

You can preserve the audio and video portions of a meeting by recording some or all of the meeting. There are a number of reasons why you might want or need to record a meeting:

- You might want to record the meeting so that people who were unable to attend can still access the meeting content.

- You might need to record the meeting because of the legal requirements of your company or industry.

- You might want to use the recording for training purposes.

Recording button

Each meeting participant sees the Recording button in their meeting window toolbar.

You can start the recording manually at any point during the meeting. However, if it's crucial that you not forget to record a particular meeting, you can configure the meeting to record automatically.

You access the recording via the meeting's chat transcript. Select the recording to play it back. The recording is available as an MPEG-4 media file, which means you can share it with other people.

You access a meeting's recording via the meeting's chat transcript.

To record a meeting

1. In the meeting window toolbar, select **More actions**.

2. Select **Start recording**. Teams begins the recording and displays an information bar reminding you to let the meeting participants know the meeting is now being recorded. Each person sees a recording button in the toolbar.

To configure a meeting to record automatically

1. Set up the scheduled meeting.

2. In your Teams calendar, select the meeting and then select **Edit**.

3. Select **Meeting options**. The Meeting Options page opens in your default web browser.

4. Set the **Record automatically** switch to **On**.

5. Select **Save**.

To stop recording a meeting

- End the meeting.

Or

1. In the meeting window toolbar, select **More actions**.

2. Select **Stop recording**.

3. In the **Stop Recording?** dialog, select **Stop recording**.

To play back a recording of a meeting

1. In the Teams app bar, select **Chat** to display the Chat panel.

2. Select the meeting's chat.

3. In the **Chat** tab, select the transcript entry for the meeting recording.

To share a link to a recording

1. In the Teams app bar, select **Chat** to display the Chat panel.

2. Select the meeting's chat.

3. In the **Chat** tab, select **More actions** (...) in the upper-right corner of the transcript entry for the meeting recording.

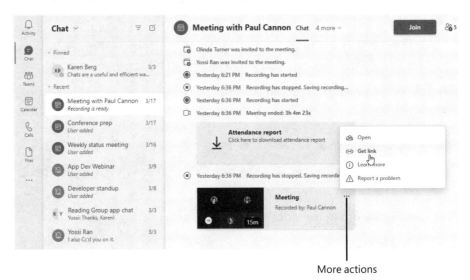

More actions

Select the recording's More Actions button, and then select Get Link.

4. Select **Get link**. Teams displays the link.

5. Select **Copy**.

6. Paste the copied link into the message you want to use to share the link, and then send the message.

Interact in meetings

Most Teams meetings consist of either conversation between the participants or the sharing of an attendee's content, such as a screen or window. However, these aren't the only ways that you can interact with the other attendees in a meeting.

For example, if someone is speaking and you want to either speak next or respond to what the person is saying, instead of interrupting or rushing to speak before someone else does, you can raise your hand. When you raise your hand during a meeting, two things happen:

- A raised-hand icon appears in the lower-left corner of your video feed.

- The same raised-hand icon appears next to your name in the **Participants** pane. Note that the raised-hand icon in the **Participants** pane has a number beside it. That number indicates the order in which hands were raised. If a second person raises a hand, that person's raised-hand icon would have a 2 inside it.

> ⚠️ **IMPORTANT** Just because you raise your hand in a meeting doesn't mean that you automatically get to speak next. In theory, the meeting organizer should honor your request and try to make sure you get to speak next. In practice, however, this often doesn't happen.

10

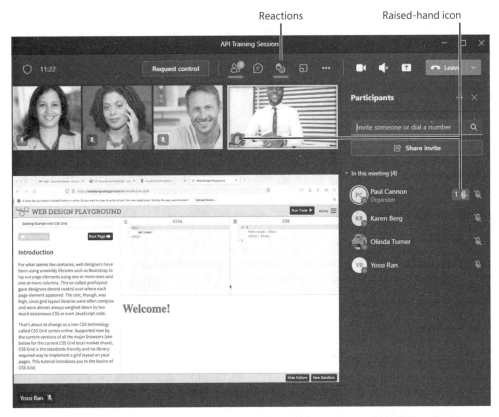

When you raise your hand in a meeting, the raised-hand icon appears with your video feed and beside your name in the Participants pane.

It isn't always necessary or efficient to respond verbally to something happening in a meeting. For example, if you like what the current speaker is saying or presenting, it might be rude or distracting to verbalize that. Rather than interrupting someone with a short comment, you can send one of the following reactions:

- Like
- Heart (love)
- Applause
- Laugh
- Surprised

The reaction appears at the bottom of the screen, floats up a short way, and then quickly disappears.

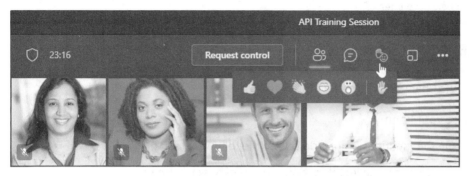

You can send one of five reactions during a meeting.

The main part of any Teams meeting is the conversation between attendees and the content that is being presented. However, one of the most important aspects of any Teams meeting is the so-called *back channel*, which is the interaction that occurs away from the main part of the meeting. The back channel happens via the meeting's Chat function, which enables all attendees to write short notes to each other and perform standard chat-related tasks such as sending emojis or animated GIFs and sharing files. And, just like a regular Teams chat, you can access the enhanced compose box to format your messages.

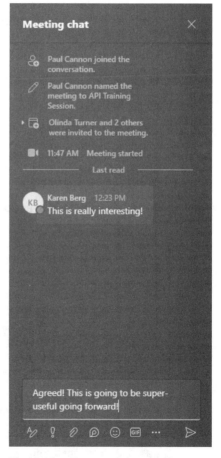

The Meeting Chat pane is home to the meeting's back channel.

10

> 🔍 **SEE ALSO** Sending chat messages in a meeting is identical to sending them using the Teams Chat app, so for details on what you can do with chat, see Chapter 7, "Chat with members of your team."

Teams displays a transcript of the meeting chat while the meeting is underway and saves that transcript after the meeting has ended. To see the meeting's chat transcript, open the Chat panel and select the meeting.

To raise your hand

- On the meeting toolbar, do one of the following:

  - **Desktop**   Select **Reactions** and then select **Raise hand**.

  - **Web**   Select **More actions** (...) and then select the **Raise hand** command.

  - **Mobile**   Select **More actions** (...) and then select the **Raise hand** button.

Or

- Press **Ctrl+Shift+K** (Windows) or **Cmd+Shift+K** (macOS).

To lower your hand

- On the meeting toolbar, do one of the following:

  - **Desktop**   Select **Reactions** and then select **Lower hand**.

  - **Web**   Select **More actions** (...) and then select the **Lower hand** command.

  - **Mobile**   Select **More actions** (...) and then select the **Lower hand** button.

Or

- Press **Ctrl+Shift+K** (Windows) or **Cmd+Shift+K** (macOS).

To send a reaction

1. Do either of the following to display the reaction buttons:

   - **Desktop**   On the meeting toolbar, select **Reactions**.

   - **Mobile**   On the meeting toolbar, select **More actions** (...) and then select **Reactions**.

2. Select the button for the type of reaction you want to send.

> **TIP** Reactions are not available in the Teams web app.

To chat during a meeting

1. Do either of the following to open the **Meeting Chat** pane:

   - **Desktop, web, or mobile (tablet)**   On the meeting toolbar, select **Chat**.

   - **Mobile (smartphone)**   On the meeting toolbar, select **More actions (...)** and then select **Chat**.

2. In the compose box at the bottom of the **Meeting Chat** pane, enter your message.

3. If you want to, format the message text or add emojis, stickers, or animated GIFs.

4. Select **Send**.

To view a meeting's chat transcript

1. In the Teams app bar, select **Chat** to display the **Chat** panel.

2. Select the meeting's chat.

Present content in meetings

Although plenty of Teams meetings are conversation-only affairs, most meetings revolve around some kind of content. For example, if the meeting is about putting together a budget, the content might be an Excel worksheet. If the meeting is about brainstorming ideas, the content might be a whiteboard where those ideas get written down. If the meeting is a training session, the content might be a website that contains the training materials.

Teams offers a wide variety of options when it comes to presenting content:

- **Screen**   Presents your entire screen, so the content is anything you open on your desktop. You also have the option of sharing your computer audio.

- **Window**   Presents just the content from a single open window. This option is only available in the desktop and web versions of the Teams app.

- **Microsoft Edge tab**   Presents just the content from a single open tab from Microsoft Edge. This option is only available in the web version of the Teams app running in Microsoft Edge.

- **Whiteboard**   Presents the same whiteboard to every attendee, and each person can use the whiteboard to write notes, draw shapes, insert images or documents, and more.

10

- **Camera**   Presents whatever content you hold up to your device camera. This option is only available in the Teams desktop app for Windows.

- **Photo or video**   Presents a photo or video that you shoot with your mobile device camera.

- **PowerPoint slideshow**   Presents the content from a PowerPoint deck.

- **File**   Presents the content from a particular file, such as a PDF.

Whatever you present, how the content itself appears depends on whose meeting window you're talking about. Here's how things look:

- For the presenter, the content itself appears on the screen and the meeting window is reduced to your video feed in the bottom-right corner. You can display the presentation controls by moving the mouse pointer to the top of the screen.

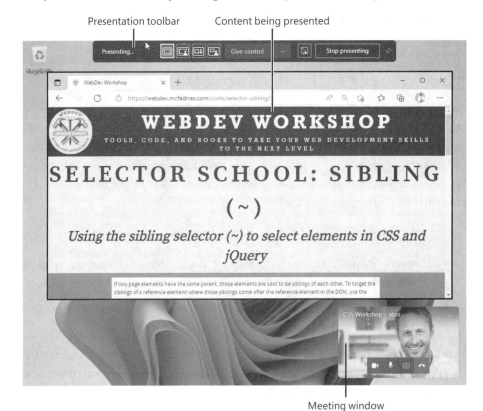

The presenter's view of a window presentation

■ For everyone else in the meeting, the content appears in the presentation area of the meeting window.

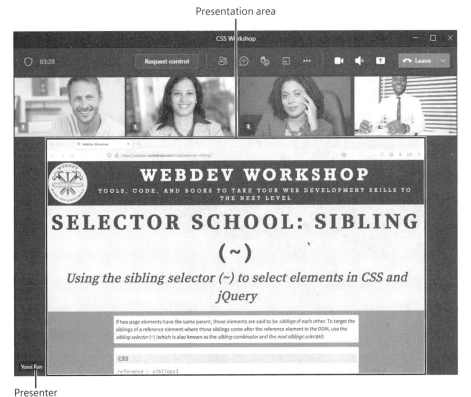

Presentation area

Presenter

A meeting with a window presentation in progress

To enhance your presentation, Teams enables you to select a *presenter mode*, which defines the relationship between the content you present and your video feed. Presenter mode is only available in the Teams desktop app for Windows, and that app offers four presenter modes:

■ **Content only** Attendees see only the content you present, which takes up the entire presentation area of the meeting window. Your video feed is not incorporated into the presentation area.

■ **Standout** Attendees see the content you present, which takes up the entire presentation area of the meeting window, as well as your video feed superimposed at the bottom of the presentation area.

- **Side-by-side**   Attendees see the content you present on the left side of the presentation area of the meeting window, and your video feed on the right of the presentation area.

- **Reporter**   Attendees see the content you present in the upper-left corner of the presentation area of the meeting window, as well as your video feed super-imposed below and to the right of the content.

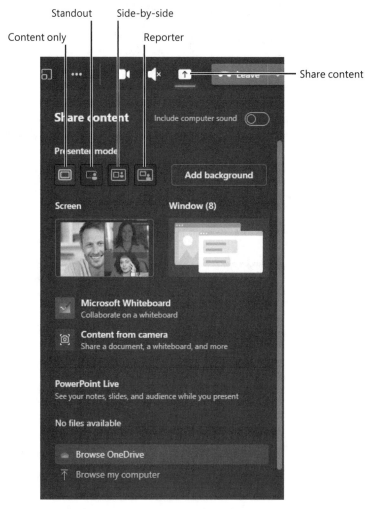

Present your content to the meeting

After you start presenting some content, someone else can request to take control of your content, or you can give control to a specified attendee.

To present your screen

1. Do either of the following to display the content sharing options:

   - **Desktop, web, or mobile for tablet**   On the meeting toolbar, select **Share content**.

   - **Mobile (smartphone)**   On the meeting toolbar, select **More actions (...)**, and then select **Share**.

   Or

   - Press **Ctrl+Shift+E** (Windows) or **Cmd+Shift+E** (macOS).

2. (Windows desktop app only) Select a presenter mode.

3. (Web app only) Select **Desktop/Window** and then select the **Entire Screen** tab.

4. (Optional) Do either of the following to include your device sound with the screen sharing:

   - **Desktop**   Set the **Include computer sound** switch to **On**.

   - **Mobile**   Set the **Audio** switch to **On**.

    TIP Sharing device sound is not available in the Teams web app.

5. Do one of the following to start sharing:

   - **Desktop**   Select **Screen**.

   - **Web**   Select **Share**.

   - **Mobile**   Select **Share screen**.

6. (Mobile app only) Select **Start Broadcast**.

To present a window

1. Do either of the following to display the content sharing options:

   - **Desktop or web**   On the meeting toolbar, select **Share content**.

   - **Desktop**   Press **Ctrl+Shift+E** (Windows) or **Cmd+Shift+E** (macOS).

    TIP Content sharing is not available in the Teams mobile app.

10

2. (Windows desktop app only) Select a presenter mode.

3. Do one of the following to display the available windows:

   - **Desktop** Select **Windows**.

   - **Web** Select **Desktop/Window** and then select the **Window** tab.

4. Do either of the following to start sharing:

   - **Desktop** Select the window you want to share.

   - **Web** Select the window you want to share, and then select **Share**.

To present a Microsoft Edge tab

1. In the Teams web app running in Microsoft Edge, display the meeting toolbar and then select **Share content**.

2. In the share tray, select **Desktop/Window**.

3. In the **Choose what to share** dialog, select the **Microsoft Edge tab** tab, select the Microsoft Edge tab you want to share, and then select **Share**.

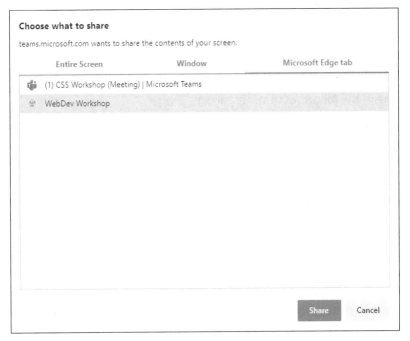

If you're running the Teams web app in Microsoft Edge, you can share an open Edge tab.

To present a whiteboard

1. Display the content sharing options:

   - **Desktop, web, or tablet**   On the meeting toolbar, select **Share content**.

   Or

   - **Desktop**   Press **Ctrl+Shift+E** (Windows) or **Cmd+Shift+E** (macOS).

2. Start sharing:

   - **Desktop**   Select **Microsoft Whiteboard**.

   - **Web**   Select **Share**.

   - **Mobile (tablet)**   Select **Share Whiteboard**.

3. Use the whiteboard tools to add text, shapes, images, and more.

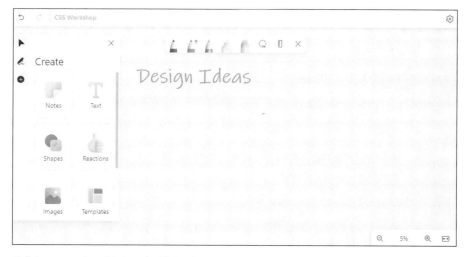

Collaborate on the whiteboard with freeform text, shapes, images, and more.

 TIP Whiteboard presentation is not available in the Teams mobile app for smartphones.

To present content through your device camera

1. On the Teams desktop app meeting toolbar, select **Content from camera**.

2. Select what you want to share through the camera:

   - **Whiteboard**   Select this option to share a physical whiteboard through the camera.

   - **Document**   Select this option to hold up a physical document to the camera.

   - **Video**   Select this option to share your camera's live video feed.

3. Share your content:

   - **Whiteboard**   Point your device camera at the physical whiteboard.

   - **Document**   Hold up the document to the camera.

   - **Video**   Point your camera at the scene where you want your live video feed to begin.

4. Select **Share**.

To present a photo or video

1. In Teams mobile app, display the content sharing options:

   - **Mobile (tablet)**   On the meeting toolbar, select **Share content**.

   - **Mobile (smartphone)**   On the meeting toolbar, select **More actions (…)**, and then select **Share**.

2. Select what you want to share:

   - **Share photo**   Select this option to share a photo that you take with your mobile device camera.

   - **Share video**   Select this option to share your mobile device camera's live video feed.

3. If you're sharing a photo, select the shutter button to take the photo.

4. Select the **Start presenting** button.

To present a PowerPoint slideshow

1. Display the content sharing options:

   - **Desktop, web, or tablet**   On the meeting toolbar, select **Share content**.

   - **Mobile (smartphone)**   On the meeting toolbar, select **More actions (…)**, and then select **Share**.

   Or

   - **Desktop**   Press **Ctrl+Shift+E** (Windows) or **Cmd+Shift+E** (macOS).

2. (Windows desktop app only) Select a presenter mode.

3. (Mobile app only) Select **Share PowerPoint**.

4. Select the PowerPoint file you want to share:

   - **Desktop**   Select either **Browse OneDrive** or **Browse My Computer**, and then select the PowerPoint file.

   - **Web**   Select **Browse**, select **Browse Teams and Channels**, **OneDrive**, or **Upload from my computer**, and then select the PowerPoint file.

   - **Mobile**   Select **OneDrive** or **Teams and channels**, and then select the PowerPoint file.

5. Run through your presentation slide show.

To present a file

1. On the meeting toolbar of the Teams desktop app or web app, select **Share content**.

2. (Windows desktop app only) Select a presenter mode.

3. Do either of the following to select the file you want to share:

   - **Desktop**   Select either **Browse OneDrive** or **Browse My Computer**, and then select the file.

   - **Web**   Select **Browse**, select **Browse Teams and Channels**, **OneDrive**, or **Upload from my computer**, and then select the file.

10

To stop presenting

- On the sharing toolbar, do either of the following:

    - **Desktop or mobile**   Select **Stop presenting**.

    - **Web**   Select **Stop sharing**.

Or

- **Desktop**   Press **Ctrl+Shift+E** (Windows) or **Cmd+Shift+E** (macOS).

To take control of a presentation (Teams desktop app only)

1. While a meeting attendee is presenting, select **Request control** in the meeting window toolbar.

2. In the **Request control?** dialog, select **Request**. Teams asks the presenter for permission for you to take control of the presentation.

To give control of a presentation (Teams desktop app only)

- If a meeting participant asks for permission to take control of your presentation, select **Allow**.

- Move the mouse pointer to the top of the presenting screen to display the toolbar, select **Give control**, and then select the name of the attendee to whom you want to give control of the presentation.

Manage breakout rooms

A small meeting is usually an efficient way to discuss an issue or disseminate information. However, once your meetings get past a certain size—that size depends on many factors but is usually between 12 and 20 participants—things become noticeably less efficient because there are just too many people trying to get screentime.

If you use the Teams desktop app, one relatively straightforward way to make a large meeting more efficient and productive is by furnishing the meeting with multiple breakout rooms. A *breakout room* is a separate meeting session that consists of some subset of the attendees from the full meeting. The number of attendees in that subset usually depends on the size of the main meeting, but it's usually from two to six participants.

To create breakout rooms (desktop app only)

1. On the meeting toolbar, select **Rooms**.

2. In the **Create breakout rooms** dialog, in the **Create rooms** list, select the number of breakout rooms (from 1 to 50) you want to add to the meeting.

3. Choose how you want to assign participants to the breakout rooms:

   • **Automatically**   Select this option to have Teams assign attendees randomly to each of your breakout rooms.

   • **Manually**   Select this option to assign attendees to each of your breakout rooms yourself.

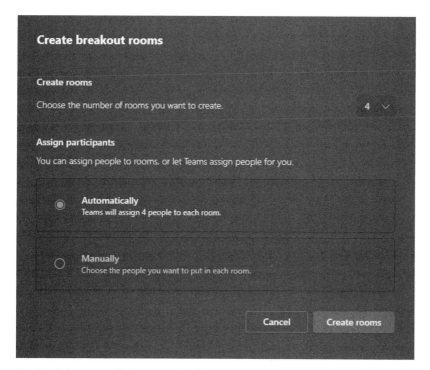

Use this dialog to specify how many breakout rooms you want to create.

4. Select **Create rooms**.

5. If you elected to manually assign attendees to the breakout rooms, Teams displays a list of attendees. For each attendee, select the breakout room (Room 1, Room 2, and so on) you want that attendee to use. When you're done, select **Assign**.

To rename a breakout room

1. On the meeting toolbar, select **Rooms**.

2. In the **Breakout Rooms** pane, to the right of the breakout room name, select **More options (...)**, and then select **Rename**.

3. Enter the new breakout room name, and then select **Rename**.

To open a breakout room

1. On the meeting toolbar, select **Rooms**.

2. In the **Breakout Rooms** pane, to the right of the breakout room name, select **More options (...)**, and then select **Open**.

To open or close all breakout rooms

1. On the meeting toolbar, select **Rooms**.

2. In the **Breakout Rooms** pane, select **Open** or **Close**.

Close a meeting

If you're presence is no longer required at a meeting, or if you joined a meeting accidentally, you can leave the meeting at any time. If you're the meeting organizer, when the meeting is complete, you'll usually want to end the meeting. (Ending the meeting is optional, however. If some of the meeting participants want to continue, you can leave the meeting, and the last person to leave will automatically end the meeting.)

To leave a meeting

- On the meeting toolbar, select **Leave**.

- Press **Ctrl+Shift+H** (Windows) or **Cmd+Shift+H** (macOS).

To end a meeting

1. On the meeting toolbar, open the **Leave** menu, and then select **End meeting**.

2. In the **End meeting?** dialog, select **End**.

Key points

- If someone misses your meeting, you can record the meeting so that person can view it later.

- If you find that you always record your meetings, you can save yourself a step by setting up your meetings to record automatically.

- If you want to speak next in a meeting, it's polite to raise your hand rather than interrupt the current speaker.

- If you like or appreciate something someone has just said, or find something humorous, there's no need to interrupt the meeting with a verbal comment. Instead, post the appropriate reaction, such as a Like, Heart, or Laugh.

- Do make full use of a meeting's back channel by using the Chat feature to post comments, asides, links, or files related to the meeting.

- Teams offers a wide variety of presentation options, including your screen, a window, an Edge tab, a whiteboard, a photo or video, and a PowerPoint slideshow.

- If you have a large meeting, consider using breakout rooms to make it easier for attendees to interact with each other and share information.

10

Make calls

Microsoft Teams is a communication and collaboration platform, so it's no surprise that Teams offers multiple ways to reach out to other people on your team, in your organization, or anywhere in the world. Depending on your version of Teams, you can post messages to team channels, you can participate in private or group chats, and you can attend virtual meetings to talk, chat, and share content.

But these aren't the only ways that Teams enables you to communicate. The business and enterprise versions of Teams are also designed to be full-fledged telephone systems that enable you to have one-on-one video or voice calls with anyone in your organization or, with the right license, anyone in the world.

This chapter introduces you to the Calls app and guides you through procedures related to setting up your Teams voicemail and checking that voicemail for messages. You also learn how to receive incoming video or voice calls and how to initiate video or voice calls.

In this chapter

- Get started with the Calls app
- Manage your Teams voicemail
- Manage incoming audio and video calls
- Manage outgoing audio and video calls

Get started with the Calls app

When you need a quick conversation with someone in your organization, or when you feel that an interaction with someone requires a bit more nuance and subtlety than a chat, consider calling that person. You can call people in Teams by using the Calls app, which enables you to make two kinds of calls:

- **Video** This is a call that includes both a video and a voice feed.

- **Audio** This is a call that includes only a voice feed.

Calls versus meetings

One of the most important things to understand about Teams calls is that they're essentially no different than meetings. That is, whether you're on a video call or a voice call, many of the same features and options that are available in a meeting are also available in a call. The features available in a call include the following:

- The Participants (or People) area, where you can add people to the call as well as pin a user and hide your own feed

- The Chat area, where you can exchange chat messages with the other person (or people) on the call

- The Share area, where you can share your screen, a window, a PowerPoint slideshow, and more

- Options such as device settings, gallery view, background effects, live captions, toggling notifications, and toggling incoming video

Because these features work the same in a call as they do in a meeting, I won't cover them again in this chapter. See Chapter 9, "Attend a meeting," and Chapter 10, "Get things done in meetings" for more information.

The Calls app enables you to search for someone to call and maintains a History section that shows your most recent incoming and outgoing calls. In the Teams desktop and web apps, Calls also shows a list of recent callers, and you can add people you frequently call to the Speed Dial section. In the desktop and web apps, Calls also has a Contacts tab, which is populated with entries from your Outlook account's Contacts folder.

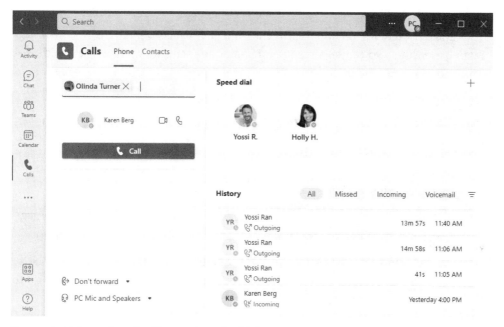

You use the Calls app to make video or voice calls with Teams.

In the lower-left corner of the Calls screen in the desktop and web app, you can configure two settings:

- **Forwarding**   The default value is Don't forward, which means that Teams rings you each time a call comes in; the alternative is Forward to voicemail, which means that Teams doesn't ring you when a call comes in; instead, Teams sends the call directly to your voicemail. You can also select More Settings in this list to open the Settings dialog with the Calls tab displayed to see extra calling options.

> **TIP** One of the extra settings is the number of seconds that Teams lets an incoming call ring before sending it to voicemail. The default is 20 seconds, but you can also choose 10, 30, 40, 50, or 60 seconds.

11

- **Audio Devices**   Select this setting to choose which connected microphone and speaker set you want to use for calling. You can also select Device settings in this list to open the Settings dialog with the Devices tab displayed to see extra device options.

Manage your Teams voicemail

In this age of instant messaging, Teams chat and channel conversations, and instant meetings, leaving a voicemail message for someone seems more than a little old-fashioned. However, the business and enterprise Teams subscriptions come with voicemail as a free part of the Calls app, so you might as well set it up and use it.

What's involved in setting up voicemail depends on which Teams app you're using:

- **Desktop or web**   You need to configure some voicemail settings, and you can optionally record a custom personal greeting if you don't want to use the Teams default greeting.

- **Mobile**   Voicemail is set up, but you need to enable it. You can also optionally record a custom personal greeting instead of using Teams' default greeting.

If you use the Teams desktop or web app, you can further configure your voicemail with *call answer rules*, which determine how you want Teams to handle calls that go to voicemail. You have five options:

- **Let the caller record a message**   This is the default setting, and it plays your personal greeting before enabling the caller to leave a message on your voicemail.

- **Let the caller record a message or be transferred to someone else**   Select this option to give the caller a choice of either leaving you a message or pressing 0 to be transferred to a person you specify.

- **End the call without playing your greeting** Select this option to skip your personal greeting and end the call without giving the caller a chance to leave a voicemail message.

- **Play your greeting and end the call**   Select this option to play your personal greeting and then end the call without giving the caller a chance to leave a voicemail message.

- **Transfer the call to someone else**   Select this option to transfer the call to a person you specify.

If you never check your messages

Are you someone who rarely, if ever, checks your voicemail for messages? Or, even if you do occasionally check your messages, are you someone who rarely, if ever, follows up on whatever the caller asks of you? If you answered "Yes" to either question, there's no need to be ashamed: Many people think voicemail is an anachronistic waste of time and treat it accordingly.

There's nothing wrong with looking at voicemail that way, but you need to be honest with your callers upfront. This means doing two things:

- Record a greeting that explicitly says you don't check voicemail and tells the caller the best way to reach you (email, Teams chat, or whatever).

- Configure your Teams call answer rules to play your greeting and then end the call without sending the caller to voicemail.

After you configure voicemail, the way you access your messages depends on the Teams app:

- **Desktop or web**   When you select Calls in the app bar, the Calls screen includes a History list that displays all your incoming and outgoing calls. A missed incoming call where the caller left a message includes the Voicemail flag. Note, too, that you can filter the History list to show only those calls with voicemail messages by selecting the Voicemail filter that appears above the list.

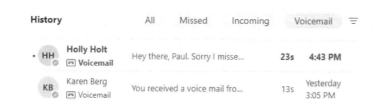

The History list shows voicemail messages.

- **Mobile**   The Calls screen includes a Voicemail button that you can select to see a list of all your voicemail messages. When you have new messages, the Voicemail button shows a red badge.

11

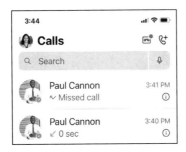

A red badge on the Voicemail button indicates new messages

After you access your voicemail list, you can select a message to play it; or, in the desktop and web apps, you can read a transcript of the message. You can also delete any voicemail you no longer need.

To configure voicemail (desktop and web apps only)

1. Select **Settings and more (...)** and then select **Settings**.

2. On the **Calls** page, select **Configure voicemail**.

3. In the **Voicemail** dialog, make a selection from the **Call answer rules** list to indicate how you want Teams to handle calls that go to voicemail.

You use the Voicemail dialog to configure your voicemail settings and record a greeting.

4. Select **Record a greeting**. Teams calls your voicemail.

> ✅ **TIP** Rather than recording a greeting, you can provide Teams with a typed greeting that Teams will play as text-to-speech. In the **Text-to-Speech Customized Greeting Option** section, use the **Your custom greeting** text box to type your greeting.

> ⚠️ **IMPORTANT** You can't use the text-to-speech customized greeting if you've already recorded a personal greeting. To delete your recorded greeting, select **Record a greeting**, press **2** to change your greeting, press **1** to listen to your greeting, press **3** to delete your greeting, and then press * to exit.

5. Follow the prompts to record and save a personal greeting.

To change your voicemail greeting (iOS and iPadOS mobile apps only)

1. Select your avatar in the upper-left corner of the Teams screen and then select **Settings**.
2. Select **Calling**.
3. Select **Change voicemail greeting**. Teams calls your voicemail.
4. Follow the prompts to record and save a personal greeting.

To enable voicemail in the mobile app (iOS and iPadOS only)

1. Select your avatar in the upper-left corner of the screen.
2. Select **Settings**.
3. Select **Calling**.
4. Leave (or select, if needed) the **Call forwarding** switch **Off**.
5. Select **If unanswered**.
6. Select **Voicemail**.

To forward incoming calls to voicemail in the mobile app (iOS and iPadOS only)

1. Select your avatar in the upper-left corner of the screen.
2. Select **Settings**.
3. Select **Calling**.

11

4. Set the **Call forwarding** switch to **On**. Teams activates call forwarding and auto-matically selects Voicemail in the Forward to list.

Incoming calls

Call forwarding

Forward to   Voicemail >

Voicemail

Change voicemail greeting

Voicemails will show in the calling app with audio playback and transcript.

In the Calling screen, set the Call Forwarding switch to On.

To check your voicemail (desktop and web apps)

1. In the Teams app bar, select **Calls**.

2. (Optional) Select the **Voicemail** filter to show only those calls that have voicemails.

3. Select the call that contains the voicemail. Teams opens the **Details** screen for the message.

4. Do one of the following:

   • In the **Voicemail** section, read the voicemail transcript.

   • Listen to the voicemail by selecting the **Play** button at the bottom of the Details screen.

To check your voicemail (mobile app)

1. On the **Calls** screen, select the **Voicemail** button.

2. On the **Voicemail** screen, select the voicemail you want to hear.

3. Select the **Play** button.

To delete a voicemail (desktop and web apps)

1. In the Teams app bar, select **Calls**.

2. (Optional) Select the **Voicemail** filter to show only those calls that have voicemails.

3. In the call that contains the voicemail, select **More actions** (...), and then select **Delete**. Teams deletes the voicemail.

To delete a voicemail (mobile app)

1. On the **Calls** screen, select the **Voicemail** button.

2. On the **Voicemail** screen, select the voicemail you want to delete, and then select the **Delete** button (the trashcan).

3. In the confirmation message box, select **Delete**.

Manage incoming audio and video calls

When a call comes in for you, what you see depends on which version of the Teams app you're using. If you're using the desktop or web app, you see a notification that tells you who is calling, displays that person's Teams avatar, and presents three buttons:

- **Accept with audio**   Answers the incoming call and sets up your end of the call as audio-only. Note that your caller might be audio-only or audio and video.

- **Accept with video**   Answers the incoming call and sets up your end of the call as audio and video. Note that your caller might be audio-only or audio and video.

- **Decline call**   Doesn't answer the call but instead sends it directly to your voicemail.

11

The notification that appears in the
Teams desktop or web app when you
receive an incoming call.

> ✅ **TIP** In the desktop and web apps, you can customize the ringtone that Teams plays when an incoming call is detected. Select **Settings and more**, select **Settings**, select **Calls**, and then use the **Calls for you** list to select the ringtone you want to use.

If you're using the Teams mobile app, the notification includes the name of the caller, the type of call (audio or video), and two buttons:

- **Accept call** Answers the incoming call and sets up your call type to be the same as the caller's. For example, if the person initiated the call as audio-only, then Teams uses only audio on your end.

- **Decline call** Doesn't answer the call but instead sends it directly to your voicemail.

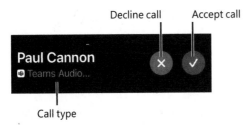

The notification that appears in the Teams mobile app when you receive an incoming call.

To accept an incoming call with audio (desktop and web apps only)

- In the call notification, select the **Accept with audio** button.
- Press **Ctrl+Shift+S** (Windows) or **Cmd+Shift+S** (macOS).

To accept an incoming call with video (desktop and web apps only)

- In the call notification, select the **Accept with video** button.
- Press **Ctrl+Shift+A** (Windows) or **Cmd+Shift+A** (macOS).

To accept an incoming call (mobile app)

- In the call notification, select the **Accept call** button.

To decline an incoming call

- **All apps** In the call notification, select the **Decline call** button.
- **Desktop and web apps** Press **Ctrl+Shift+D** (Windows) or **Cmd+Shift+D** (macOS).

Manage outgoing audio and video calls

When you want to make a call through Teams, your choices are quite simple:

- **Audio call** This is an audio-only call, although note that the person you call might answer as a video call.

- **Video call** This is a call that uses both audio and video, although note that the person you call might answer as a voice (audio-only) call.

> ⚠ **IMPORTANT** This section only covers making calls to people in your organization, which is available to all users who have a paid Teams subscription. For more advanced calling features, such as the capability of dialing numbers outside your organization, you need an add-on Teams license. See your Teams administrator.

To make an audio call (desktop or web app)

- In the **Calls** panel, use the **Type a name** text box to type the name of the person you want to call, select the person in the search results, and then select **Call**.

- Select **Calls** in the app bar, hover the mouse pointer over the person in the **Speed dial** section, and then select the **Audio call** button. To add a person to the **Speed dial** section, select **Add** (+), start typing the person's name, select the name in the search results, and then select **Add**.

11

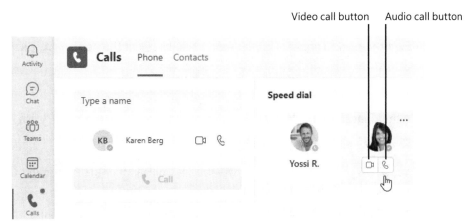

Video call button   Audio call button

Point to a Speed Dial contact to display call buttons.

- Select **Calls** in the app bar, select the **Contacts** tab, and then select the **Audio call** button for the person you want to call.

- Select **Calls** in the app bar, hover the mouse pointer over a call to or from the person in the **History** list, and then select **Call**.

- Display the person's contact card (in, for example, the **Chat** pane) and then select the **Audio call** button.

- In the Teams **Search** box, type /call, start typing the name of the person you want to call, and then select the person's name in the search results.

To make an audio call (mobile app)

1. On the **Calls** screen, select the **Make a call** button.

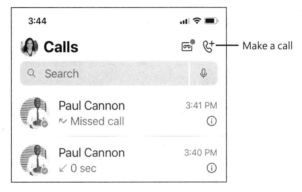

Select the Make a Call button to make a call using the Teams mobile app

2. Start typing the name of the person you want to call.

3. When the person appears in the search results, select the person's **Audio call** button.

Or

- On the **Calls** screen, select a call to or from the person in the **History** list.

To make a video call (desktop or web app)

- Select **Calls** in the app bar, hover the mouse pointer over the person in the **Speed dial** section, and then select the **Video call** button.

- Select **Calls** in the app bar, select the **Contacts** tab, and then select the **Video call** button for the person you want to call.

- Display the person's contact card (in, for example, the **Chat** pane) and then select the **Video call** button.

To make a video call (mobile app)

1. On the **Calls** screen, select the **Make a call** button.

2. Start typing the name of the person you want to call.

3. When the person appears in the search results, select the person's **Video call** button.

Key points

- A standard Teams license enables you to make and receive calls between members of your organization.

- If you want to call people outside your organization, you need an add-on phone license that supports this feature.

- With Teams, you can make either video calls, which include both audio and video feeds, or audio calls, which include only an audio feed.

- Use the Calls app to view your history of incoming and outgoing calls, access your voicemail, and initiate audio or video calls.

11

Customize Teams

Microsoft Teams works well right out of the box (so to speak), so you might go your entire Teams career without changing any of the default settings in whatever version (or versions) of the app you use.

That said, you shouldn't ignore the customization settings that Teams offers because you never know when a particular setting might come in handy. For example, if you find yourself regularly using Teams in low-light situations, you might find Teams easier to read and easier on your eyes if you switch to dark mode. Similarly, if you dislike the read receipts that Teams sends to let people know when you've seen the messages they send to you, you can disable the read receipts to enhance your privacy. These and many other customizations are available through the collection of settings available in the Teams app.

This chapter introduces you to the Teams Settings feature and guides you through procedures related to customizing the Teams appearance, privacy settings, notifications, and app permissions.

In this chapter

- Access Teams settings
- Change the theme
- Customize privacy settings
- Customize notifications
- Customize app permissions

Access Teams settings

The experience of working with settings in Teams varies depending on which Teams app you use.

The desktop and web versions of the Teams app use the same interface and offer mostly the same set of options (with the glaring difference being the device settings that are available on the desktop but not the web). In both the desktop and web versions of Teams, you modify the settings using the Settings dialog, which offers a set of categories on the left, with the settings available in the selected category on the right. In both apps, a setting goes into effect as soon as you change it or select it.

> **SEE ALSO** I don't cover the device settings in this chapter because I already discussed them earlier in the "Manage audio and video devices" section of Chapter 9, "Attend a meeting."

The Settings dialog from the Teams Windows app

In the mobile versions of the Teams app, you customize the settings using either the Settings screen on an Android or iOS smartphone or the Settings dialog on a tablet device. The mobile settings overlap somewhat with those in the desktop and web apps, but you generally have fewer customization options in the mobile app.

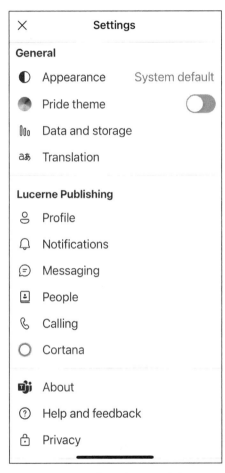

The Settings screen from the Teams iPhone app

To open the Settings dialog in the desktop or web app

- To the left of your Teams account profile button, select **Settings and more** (...), and then select **Settings**.

- (Desktop app only) Press **Ctrl+,** (comma; Windows) or **Cmd+,** (comma; macOS).

To access settings in the mobile app

- In the upper-left corner of the app, select your Teams account profile button, and then select **Settings**.

> ⚠ **IMPORTANT** There are slight differences in the layout and the available settings between the Android app's Settings screen, the iPhone app's Settings screen, and the tablet app's Settings dialog.

Change the theme

The *theme* is an overall look applied to each element in the Teams app. Teams doesn't offer a wide range of these customizations. In the desktop and web apps, for example, you have just three choices for the theme:

- **Default** This is the theme that's applied to Teams when you start using the app, and it uses dark text on a light background.

- **Dark** This theme uses mostly light text on a dark background.

- **High contrast** This theme uses bright foreground colors and dark background colors, similar to the high-contrast themes that are available for Windows. Use the High contrast theme if you find that Teams screen elements look blurry or blend together using the Default or Dark theme.

SETTINGS   THEME

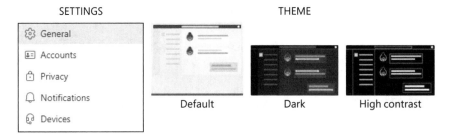

Default   Dark   High contrast

The three theme settings available in the Teams desktop and web apps

The Teams mobile app also offers only three theme settings:

- **Light** This theme uses mostly dark text on a light background.

- **Dark** This theme uses mostly light text on a dark background.

- **System default** This option tells Teams to switch to the Light or Dark theme automatically to match the current operating system display mode. For example, if you change your iPhone to Dark mode (by selecting Settings, Display & Brightness, Dark), Teams automatically switches to the Dark theme.

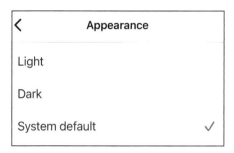

The three theme settings available from the Teams mobile app

To change the theme in the desktop app or web app

1. Open the **Settings** dialog.

2. On the **General** page, select the **Default**, **Dark**, or **High contrast** theme.

To change the theme in the mobile app

- On the **Settings** screen, select **Appearance** and then select **Light**, **Dark**, or **System default**.

> **TIP** While you're in the **General** category of the desktop or web app, note that you can also customize the appearance of your chat conversations. Select **Comfy** to get extra space between messages and to display your messages on the right and your recipient's messages on the left. To see more messages, select **Compact**; doing so changes the view so that there's less space between messages and aligns all messages on the left.

12

Customize privacy settings

Since you likely use Teams in a work setting, privacy isn't usually a major concern. However, that doesn't mean that you should ignore privacy completely. For example, many people dislike the notification that Teams displays to the sender of a message when you read that message. Similarly, you might have one or more unwanted callers that you'd prefer not to hear from. The next few sections cover these and other privacy-related Teams settings.

Allow priority access during Do not disturb

When your Teams status is set to Do not disturb, Teams disables all notifications for activities such as incoming chat and channel messages, personal @mentions, replies to conversations you're in, likes and reactions to your posts, incoming phone calls, and more.

 SEE ALSO For information about Do not disturb and other Teams statuses, see "Set your status" in Chapter 1, "Get started with Teams."

Do not disturb is a great way to focus on your work, but there might be one or more people that you want to hear from, no matter what. You can customize your privacy settings in the desktop or web app to give those people *priority access*, which means their notifications come through even when your status is set to Do not disturb.

To add someone to your priority access list

1. Open the **Settings** dialog.

2. On the **Privacy** page, select **Manage priority access**.

3. In the **Add people** box, start typing the person's name or number.

4. When the person's name appears in the search result, select the name.

5. Repeat steps 3 and 4 for each person you want to give priority access.

To remove someone from your priority access list

1. Open the **Settings** dialog.

2. On the **Privacy** page, select **Manage priority access**.

3. In the **Manage priority access** dialog, select **Delete** (**X**) to the right of the person you want to remove from the priority access list.

Block unwanted phone numbers

If you're receiving external phone calls that are unnecessary, irritating, or even abusive, you can block the phone number of the caller. Teams also enables you to block all incoming calls that have no caller ID.

To block calls with no caller ID

1. Open the **Settings** dialog or screen in your Teams app.

2. Select a **Settings** category:

   - **Desktop** Select **Privacy**.

   - **Web** Select **Privacy**.

   - **Mobile** Select **Calling**.

3. Select the **Block calls with no caller ID** checkbox.

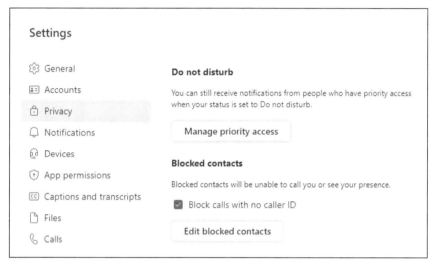

Select the Block Calls with No Caller ID checkbox.

To block a phone number (desktop or web app)

1. In the Teams app bar, select **Calls**.

2. Select the **Contacts** tab.

3. Select **Add contact**.

4. Enter the phone number you want to block, select the number in the search results, and then select **Add**.

5. To the right of the number you just added, select **More actions** (...), and then select **Block**.

12

Select the contact's More Actions button, and then select Block.

To block a phone number (mobile app)

1. On the **Settings** screen, select **Calling**.

2. On the **Calling** screen, select **Blocked numbers**.

3. In the **Blocked Numbers** dialog, select **Add number**.

4. Enter the phone number you want to block, and then select **Block**.

To unblock a phone number (desktop or web app)

1. In the Teams app bar, select **Calls**.

2. Select the **Contacts** tab.

3. To the right of the number you no longer want to block, select **More actions** (...), and then select **Unblock**.

Or

1. Open the **Settings** dialog.

2. Select **Privacy**.

3. Select **Edit blocked contacts**. Teams displays the **Manage Blocked People** window.

4. To the right of the phone number you no longer want to block, select **Unblock**. Teams removes the phone number from the **Manage Blocked People** window.

To unblock a phone number (mobile app)

1. On the **Settings** screen, select **Calling**.

2. On the **Calling** screen, select **Blocked numbers**.

3. In the **Blocked Numbers** dialog, select **Edit**.

4. Select the red delete button to the left of the phone number you no longer want to block, and then select **Delete**. Teams removes the phone number from the **Blocked Numbers** list.

5. Select **Done**.

Turn off read receipts

By default, when you send a message to someone, and that person views your message, Teams displays the Seen icon (an eyeball) to the right of the message to let you know that your message has been read. Displaying the Seen icon is the Teams version of a read receipt (that is, a notification that lets you know when your recipient has read a message you sent).

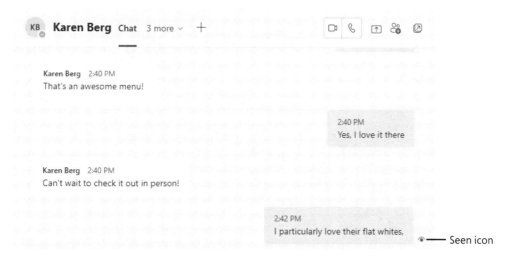

Teams displays the Seen icon when your recipient reads your message.

Most of the time, the Seen icon is harmless, but some people dislike it because it sets up the expectation that now that the message has been seen, then surely a response should arrive soon. If you don't want your recipients to know when you've read their messages, you can turn off read receipts, which means Teams no longer displays the Seen icon when you read a message.

To turn off read receipts

1. Open the **Settings** dialog or screen in your Teams app.

2. Select a Settings category:

   - **Desktop**   Select **Privacy**.

   - **Web**   Select **Privacy**.

   - **Mobile**   Select **Messaging**.

3. Set the **Read receipts** switch to **Off**.

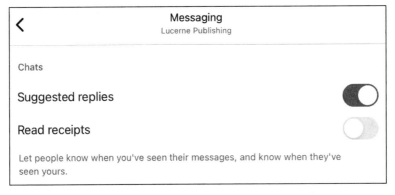

Set the Read Receipts switch to Off.

Customize notifications

One way that Teams fosters a sense of community, enhances team cohesion, and improves collaboration is through the liberal use of notifications. A *notification* is an on-screen indication of a specific Teams activity. These notifications come in four styles:

- A temporary banner message in the lower-right corner of the screen (for the desktop and web apps) or at the top of the screen (for the mobile app)

- A message added to your Activity feed

- A badge over an icon (such as the Activity icon in the app bar or a channel in the Teams panel)

- A sound played through your device speakers or headphones

Teams notifications are useful not only because you have multiple ways to learn about recent activity but also because Teams displays notifications for a wide array of events, including the following:

- When a message arrives for a chat in which you're a participant

- When a post is added to a channel of which you're a member

- When someone likes or reacts to one of your messages or posts

- When someone @mentions you, a team you belong to, or a channel you follow

- When someone calls you

However, when it comes to notifications, one person's useful is another person's annoying. That is, you might find that Teams brings a bit *too* much gusto to its notifications. If that's the case, Teams has your back because it offers fine-grained control over not only the types of notifications you see but also the events that generate notifications.

12

To customize notifications (desktop or web app)

1. Open the **Settings** dialog or screen in your Teams app.

2. Select the **Notifications** category. Teams displays its notification settings.

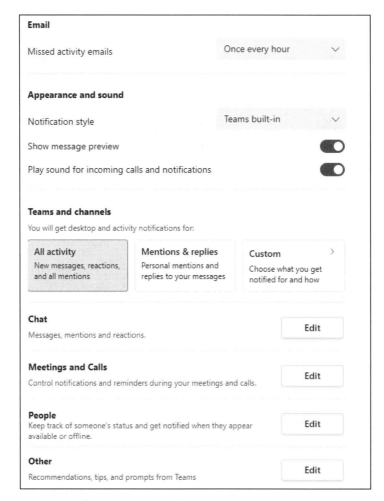

Select the Notifications category in the Settings dialog.

3. If you don't want Teams to send you an email when you miss an activity, use the **Missed activity emails** list to select **Off**. Otherwise, select the time interval you want Teams to wait for you to check your new activity before sending you a reminder email (the default is **Once every hour**).

4. (Desktop app only) If you want Teams to use the notifications system of your device operating system instead of Teams' built-in notifications, use the **Notification style** list to select **Windows** (Windows) or **Mac** (macOS).

5. For chat or post notifications, if you don't want the banner to include the first few words of the message, set the **Show message preview** switch to **Off**.

6. If you don't want Teams to play a sound along with its notifications, set the **Play sound for incoming calls and notifications** switch to **Off**.

7. Select the notification level you want for your teams and channels:

   - **All activity** Select this level to see both a banner and activity feed notification for all your team and channel events.

   - **Mentions and replies** Select this level to see both a banner and activity feed notification for just your personal @mentions and replies to your posts.

   - **Custom** Select this level to customize your team and channel notifications using the Custom window. To shut off notifications for a particular event, use the event's list to select **Off**. (Note that **Off** isn't an option for the **Personal @mentions** event.) Otherwise, select either **Banner and feed** (that is, you see both a banner notification and an activity feed notification) or **Only show in feed** (that is, you just see an activity feed notification).

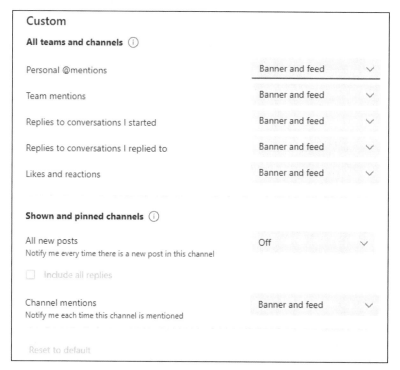

In the Notifications category, select Custom to customize your Teams notifications.

12

8. In the **Chat** section, select **Edit** to see a list of chat-related events, each of which has a list in which you can select how you want to be notified. In most cases, you see three options: **Off**, **Banner and feed**, and **Only show in feed**.

9. In the **Meetings and Calls** section, select **Edit** to customize notifications for Teams meetings and phone calls.

10. In the **People** section, select **Edit** to add notifications for when specific people have their status change to Available or Offline.

11. In the **Other** section, select **Edit** to customize miscellaneous notifications, such as when someone you know joins Teams.

To customize notifications (mobile app)

1. On the **Settings** screen, select **Notifications**.

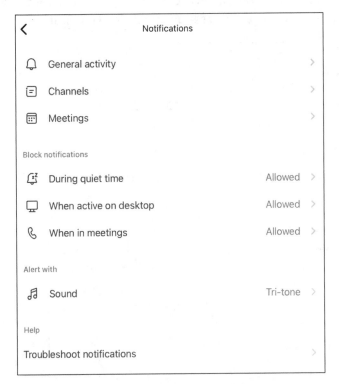

Select the Notifications category in the Settings dialog or screen

2. On the **Notifications** screen, select **General activity**.

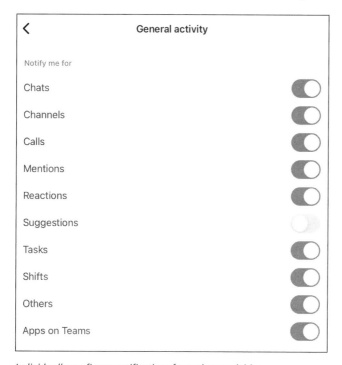

Individually configure notifications for various activities.

3. For each activity, turn off the toggle for each type of event for which you don't want to get notified. Select **Back** (<) when you're done.

4. On the **Notifications** screen, select **Meetings**.

5. On the **Meetings** screen, select whether you want to be notified when meetings start and whether you want meeting chats muted:

   • **Meeting start reminder** Select **All meetings, Accepted meetings only**, or **None**.

   • **Meeting chat** Select **Unmute, Mute until I join or send a message**, or **Mute**.

6. To mute notifications on a schedule, on the **Notifications** screen, select **During quiet time**, and then set your schedule using one or both of the following:

   - **Daily quiet hours**   Turn on this toggle and then specify the **Start** and **End** times between which you want all Teams notifications to be muted.

   - **Quiet days**   Turn on this toggle and then select the full days you want all Teams notifications to be muted.

7. To mute mobile app notifications when you're active in the Teams desktop app, on the **Notifications** screen, select **When active on desktop** and then turn on the **When active on desktop** toggle.

> **IMPORTANT** Teams considers you inactive when you haven't interacted with the app for at least five minutes (iOS and iPadOS) or at least three minutes (Android).

8. To mute notifications when you're in Teams meetings, on the **Notifications** screen, select **When in meetings** and then turn on the **When in meetings** toggle.

9. If you don't want Teams to play a sound along with its notifications, select **Sound** and then select **None**.

Customize app permissions

If you use apps within your Teams environment, you can gain more control over your privacy by setting specific permissions on what the app is allowed to do and what resources the app is allowed to access. How you set app permissions depends on which Teams app you use:

- **Desktop**   The specific permissions required by an app vary but can include some or all of the following:

  - **Media**   Gives the app permission to access your computer's camera, microphone, and speakers.

  - **Location**   Gives the app permission to access your current location.

  - **Notifications**   Gives the app permission to display notifications.

  - **MIDI device**   Gives the app permission to access a MIDI keyboard or similar digital music instrument connected to your computer.

  - **External links**   Gives the app permission to link to sites outside of your organization.

- **Web** The permissions are the same as with the desktop app, but you must make sure that your browser's permissions are configured to match. For example, if you allow an app access to your camera, you must configure your browser with permission to access the camera.

- **Mobile** The mobile app doesn't offer specific app permissions. Instead, Teams uses the app permissions that you configure in the device settings:

  - **Android** Select **Settings**, **Privacy**, and then **Permission Manager**.

  - **iOS or iPadOS** Select **Settings**, and then **Privacy**.

To customize app permissions (desktop or web app)

1. Open the **Settings** dialog in your Teams app.

2. Select the **App permissions** category. Teams displays a list of your apps.

3. Select the app you want to work with. Teams displays the resources the app can use.

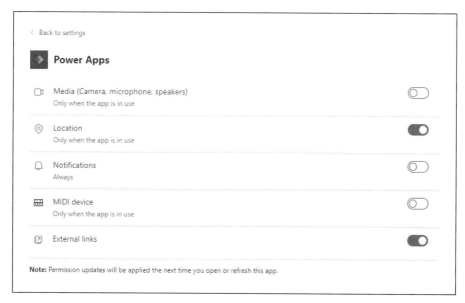

Teams enables you to choose which resources you want to allow the app to access.

4. For each resource, set its switch to **On** if you want to give the app permission to access that resource.

5. Select **Back** (<) when you're done.

Key points

- If you use Teams in a dark room, switch to the Dark theme for easier viewing.

- If you're waiting for an important message, post, or call from someone, but you don't want to be disturbed by anyone else, give that person priority access and then switch your status to Do Not Disturb.

- If you find that Teams is a little overzealous in its notifications, set up a custom notification setup that allows only those notifications that are important to you.

- To get the most out any app you use with Teams, make sure that app has the necessary permissions to perform the tasks you want.

Administer Teams

If you're a Microsoft 365 or Teams administrator for your organization, you can use the Teams admin center to view, manage, and modify your organization's Teams deployment.

The Teams admin center is a powerful tool that's home to hundreds of options and settings, dozens of policies, and a large collection of management tools. It's well beyond the scope of this book to cover the Teams admin center in detail. Instead, this chapter introduces you to the admin center and shows you how to work with the admin center in general terms by creating, editing, and assigning policies.

This chapter introduces you to the Teams admin center website and guides you through procedures related to signing in to the admin center; navigating the interface; creating custom policies; editing, duplicating, and deleting custom policies; editing and resetting Global policies; and assigning policies to users and groups.

In this chapter

- Get to know the Teams admin center
- Manage Teams via policies

Get to know the Teams admin center

All your Teams administration chores take place in the Microsoft Teams admin center, which is a collection of web pages that's part of the Microsoft 365 administration inter- face. To access either the Microsoft 365 admin center or the Microsoft Teams admin center, you need to have been assigned either of the following Microsoft 365 roles:

- Global Administrator

- Teams Administrator

These roles enable you to access and log in to the Teams admin center to view, manage, and modify your organization's Teams deployment. The following Teams- specific roles can access a subset of the Teams admin center:

- **Teams Communications Administrator**   Has access to the meeting and voice- related settings and policies within the Teams admin center

- **Teams Communications Support Engineer**   Has access to advanced tools to troubleshoot call quality problems

- **Teams Communications Support Specialist**   Has access to basic tools to troubleshot call quality problems

- **Teams Device Administrator**   Has access to the device-related settings and policies within the Teams admin center

The Teams admin center is divided into *nodes*, each of which you use to administer a specific aspect of your Teams deployment:

- Dashboard

- Teams

- Users

- Teams devices

- Teams apps

- Meetings

- Messaging policies

- Voice

- Locations

- Enhanced encryption policies

- Policy packages

- Planning

- Analytics & reports

- Notifications & alerts

To access a node, select its button on the Navigation menu on the left. Select the Navigation menu button to expand the full Navigation menu. When the Navigation menu is expanded, you see each node name as well as its icon.

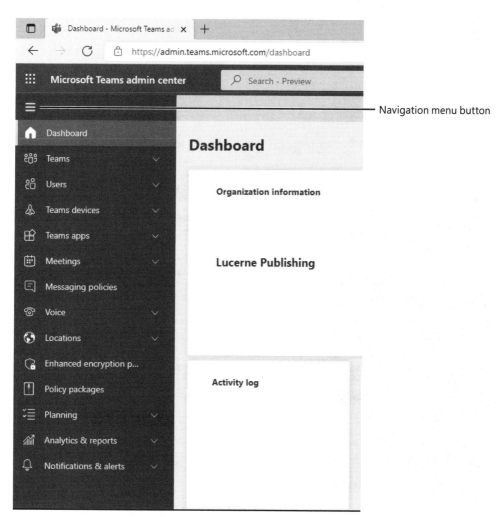

The Microsoft Teams admin center's navigation menu

When you select a node on the Navigation menu, the Teams admin center displays either a page or a submenu of commands. For example, selecting Dashboard or Messaging policies displays those pages. Selecting Teams in the navigation menu displays a submenu of the following commands:

- Manage teams
- Teams settings
- Teams policies
- Team templates
- Templates policies
- Teams update policies
- Teams upgrade settings

Selecting a command from the submenu displays that command's interface on the right side of the admin center page.

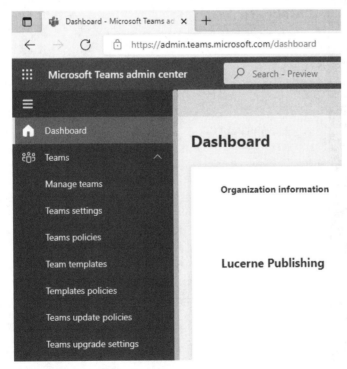

In the Teams admin center navigation menu, selecting most items displays a submenu.

The admin center's large collection of policies contains hundreds of settings that give you fine-grained control over almost every aspect of your Teams deployment. To give you a sense of what can be done with the Teams admin center, the following table offers a selection of policy settings.

Policy node	Setting	Description
Teams policies	Create private channels	Allow or deny Teams users the ability to create private channels.
Setup policies	Installed apps	Choose the apps and messaging extensions that are installed by default for each Teams user.
Setup policies	Pinned apps	Change and reorder apps on the Teams app bar and in messaging extensions.
Meeting policies	Screen sharing mode	Control desktop and application sharing during meetings.
Meeting policies	Let anonymous people join a meeting	Controls whether people outside your organization (guests) can join meetings.
Meeting policies	Meeting reactions	Hide or show the Reactions menu in meetings.
Messaging policies	Read receipts	Determines the default behavior of Teams read receipts: User controlled, Turned off for everyone, or Turned on for everyone.
Messaging policies	Giphy in conversations	Controls whether animated GIFs are available in chat and channel conversations.
Messaging policies	Suggested replies	Controls whether Teams displays suggested replies for chat messages.
Calling policies	Voicemail is available for routing inbound calls	Determines the default availability of voicemail for incoming calls: User controlled, Enabled, or Not enabled.

Most of your work in the Teams admin center involves doing one or more of the following:

- **Run a task**   You use a task to configure some aspect of your Teams deployment. For example, you can create a team, add a user, or add an app to a team.

13

- **Modify a setting**   You use settings to control global properties of your Teams deployment. For example, the Teams admin center offers several settings related to tags, including defining who can manage tags and setting up a list of suggested tags.

- **Apply a policy**   You use policies to apply a collection of settings to a user, a group, or your organization. For example, the meeting policies determine (among many other things) whether users can start instant meetings in channels, whether reactions are allowed in meetings, and which screen-sharing options are available.

To access the Teams admin center

- In a web browser, go to admin.teams.microsoft.com.

Or

1. In a web browser, go to the Microsoft 365 admin center at admin.microsoft.com.

2. In the upper-left corner, select the **Navigation menu** button.

3. At the bottom of the Navigation menu, select **Show all**.

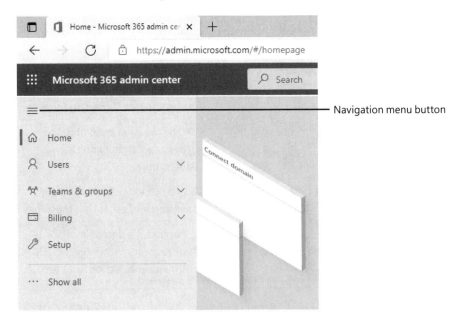

In the Microsoft 365 admin center, display the navigation menu.

4. In the **Admin centers** section of the navigation menu, select **Teams**.

Manage Teams via policies

Although the Teams admin center offers a sizable roster of tasks you can perform and settings you can modify, you'll probably spend the bulk of your Teams administration efforts setting up and applying policies. In Teams, a *policy* is a collection of settings related to some aspect of your Teams deployment and that you can apply as a whole to one or more users, to a group, or to your entire organization. The last of these is known as a *global* or *org-wide* policy. The Teams admin center offers policies for the following Teams components:

- **Teams** On the **Navigation** menu, select **Teams** and then **Teams policies**.

- **Team templates** On the **Navigation** menu, select **Teams** and then **Templates policies**.

- **Teams (and Office) preview versions** On the **Navigation** menu, select **Teams** and then **Teams update policies**.

- **App permissions** On the **Navigation** menu, select **Teams apps** and then **Permission policies**.

- **App installation** On the **Navigation** menu, select **Teams apps** and then **Setup policies**.

- **Meetings** On the **Navigation** menu, select **Meetings** and then **Meeting policies**.

- **Live events** On the **Navigation** menu, select **Meetings** and then **Live events policies**.

- **Chat and channel messages** On the **Navigation** menu, select **Messaging policies**.

- **Calling** On the **Navigation** menu, select **Voice** and then **Calling policies**.

- **Call park** On the **Navigation** menu, select **Voice** and then **Call park policies**.

- **Caller ID** On the **Navigation** menu, select **Voice** and then **Caller ID policies**.

- **Emergency calling** On the **Navigation** menu, select **Voice** and then **Emergency policies**.

- **Voice routing** On the **Navigation** menu, select **Voice** and then **Voice routing policies**.

13

Work with policies

To work with policies in the Teams admin center, you can either make changes to one of the default policies that Teams offers, or you can create your own custom policies. If you want to modify an existing policy, note that most policy-related nodes in the Teams admin center offer the following:

- **Global (Org-wide default)**   This policy contains default settings for the particular node and is applied by default for everyone in your organization.

- **Node-specific policies**   This refers to one or more policies that implement some subset of the Global policy, usually to accomplish some goal or task. For example, the **Meeting policies** node offers the following five policies (in addition to the default Global policy):

  - **AllOn**   This policy turns on every meeting-related setting.

  - **RestrictedAnonymousAccess**   This policy implements settings that restrict anonymous (guest) access to meetings.

  - **AllOff**   This policy turns off every meeting-related setting.

  - **RestrictedAnonymousNoRecording** This policy implements settings that prevent guests from recording meetings.

  - **Kiosk**   This policy sets up Teams to be used in Kiosk mode.

> ⚠ IMPORTANT Microsoft has announced that the AllOn, RestrictedAnonymousAccess, and RestrictedAnonymousNoRecording policies will one day be deprecated, so they might not be available by the time you read this.)

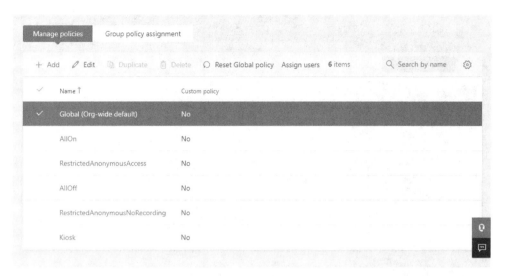

The policies available in the Meeting Policies node of the Teams admin center

Although you're free to apply any of Teams' predefined policies, note that you can only edit the Global policies (as well as any custom policies that you create).

To create a custom policy

1. On the **Navigation** menu, select the policy node you want to work with.
2. In the toolbar of the node's **Manage policies** tab, select **Add**.
3. Enter a name and description for the policy.
4. Modify the policy settings as necessary, and then at the bottom of the policy settings, select **Save**.

To edit a Global or custom policy

1. On the **Navigation** menu, select the policy node you want to work with.
2. In the node's **Manage policies** tab, select the name of the policy you want to modify.
3. Modify the policy settings as necessary, and then at the bottom of the page, select **Save**.

299

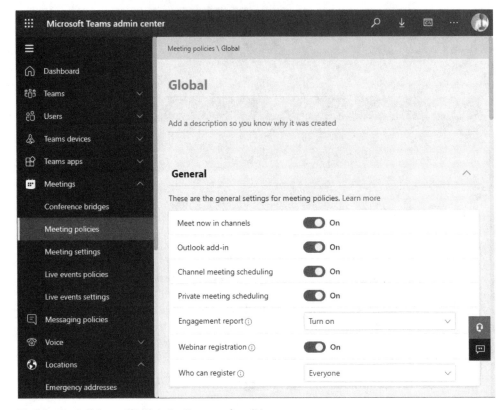

The Meeting Policies node's Global policy, open for editing

To duplicate a custom policy

1. On the **Navigation** menu, select the policy node you want to work with.

2. In the node's **Manage policies** tab, select the custom policy you want to duplicate.

>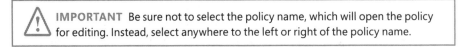
> **IMPORTANT** Be sure not to select the policy name, which will open the policy for editing. Instead, select anywhere to the left or right of the policy name.

3. In the **Manage policies** toolbar, select **Duplicate**.

4. Enter a name for the duplicate policy, and then select **Confirm**.

To delete a custom policy

1. On the **Navigation** menu, select the policy node you want to work with.

2. In the node's **Manage policies** tab, select the custom policy you want to delete.

> **IMPORTANT** Do not select the policy name, which will open the policy for editing. Instead, select anywhere to the left or right of the policy name.

3. In the **Manage policies** toolbar, select **Delete**.

4. In the confirmation message box, select **OK**.

To reset a Global policy

1. On the **Navigation** menu, select the policy node you want to work with.

2. In the node's **Manage policies** tab, select the **Global (Org-wide default)** policy.

> **IMPORTANT** Do not select the policy name, which will open the policy for editing, Instead, select anywhere to the left or right of the policy name.

3. In the **Manage policies** tab's toolbar, select **Reset Global policy**.

Assign a policy

For each Teams feature that supports policies, the Global policy for that feature is in effect by default, meaning that Teams has applied that policy across the organization. If you need custom settings for your organization, the easiest method is to edit the Global policy as needed, as described in the previous section.

However, if you need a more granular approach that applies a policy to some subset of your organization, then you need to either create a custom policy or choose a predefined Teams policy that works for your team. You then need to assign that custom or predefined policy to put it into effect.

Teams gives you three ways to assign a policy:

- Assign the policy to a user
- Assign the policy to a batch of users
- Assign the policy to a group

13

Understand policy precedence

Because Teams enables you to assign a policy on multiple levels—user (individually or in batches), group, and organization—a specific user can be "assigned" multiple levels of policy. For example, if you assign a meeting policy to a user and also assign a different meeting policy to a group of which that user is a member, then the user has been assigned three levels of policy: individual, group, and organization (via the Global meeting policy that applies organization-wide).

When a user has multiple policy levels, how does Teams know which policy to actually apply to the user? Teams determines a user's effective policy by using the following rules of precedence:

- A policy assigned to the user directly (either individually or in a batch assignment) has the highest precedence.

- A policy that the user inherits from a group assignment has the next-highest precedence.

- If the user inherits the same policy from two or more groups, the policy that has the highest group assignment ranking is given precedence. (A *group assignment ranking* is a numeric rank that you supply when you apply a policy to group.)

- A policy that the user inherits from the Global policy has the lowest precedence.

To assign a policy to a user

1. On the **Navigation** menu, select **Users** and then select **Manage users**.

2. Select the user to whom you want to assign the policy, and then select **Edit settings**.

 IMPORTANT Do not select the user's name, which will open the user's informa-tion page. Instead, select anywhere to the left or right of the user's name.

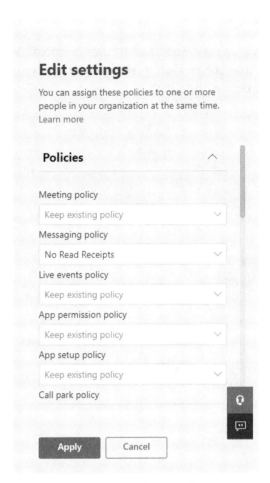

Edit settings

You can assign these policies to one or more people in your organization at the same time. Learn more

Policies ⌃

Meeting policy

Keep existing policy ⌄

Messaging policy

No Read Receipts ⌄

Live events policy

Keep existing policy ⌄

App permission policy

Keep existing policy ⌄

App setup policy

Keep existing policy ⌄

Call park policy

Apply Cancel

Use the policy node lists to select the policy you want to apply to the user.

13

3. In the **Edit settings** pane, expand the **Policies** section if necessary. Select the custom or predefined policy you want to apply to the user, and then select **Apply**.

To assign a policy to a batch of users

1. On the **Navigation** menu, select the policy node you want to work with.

2. In the node's **Manage policies** tab, select the policy you want to assign.

> ⚠ IMPORTANT Be sure not to select the policy name, which will open the policy for editing. Instead, select anywhere to the left or right of the policy name.

3. In the **Manage policies** toolbar, select **Assign users**.

4. In the **Manage users** pane, start typing the name of the user to whom you want to assign the policy. When the user appears in the search results, point to the name and then select the **Add** button.

When the user appears in the search results, select the user's Add button.

5. Repeat Step 4 as needed to add all the users to whom you want to apply the policy. Then select **Apply**.

To assign a custom policy to a group

1. On the **Navigation** menu, select the policy node you want to work with.

2. Select the node's **Group policy assignment** tab, and then select **Add**.

3. In the **Assign policy to group** pane, in the **Select a group** text box, start typing the name of the group to which you want to assign the policy. When the group appears in the search results, select that group's **Add** button.

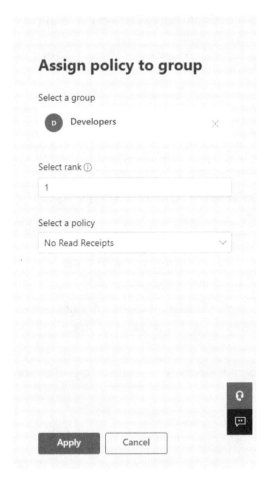

Use the Assign Policy to Group pane to assign and rank a policy for a specified group.

4. In the **Select rank** text box, enter the group assignment rank you want to use for this policy assignment.

> ⚠️ **IMPORTANT** Remember that Teams uses the group assignment rank to determine which policy has precedence when a user is a member of multiple groups that have been assigned policies for a particular Teams node. The lower the rank, the higher the precedence.

5. In the **Select a policy** list, select the custom policy you want to assign to the group.

6. Select **Apply**.

Key points

- You can have full access to the Teams admin center if you've been assigned the Microsoft 365 role of Global Administrator or Teams Administrator.

- You access the Teams admin center directly by surfing to *https://admin.teams.microsoft.com/*.

- Use the **Navigation** menu on the left to select the node you want to work with. In most cases, you select a navigation menu item to display a submenu of the available nodes, and then select the one you want.

- A policy is a collection of settings related to some aspect of your Teams deployment. Rather than applying individual settings to a user or group, you can apply the entire policy at once.

- You can apply a policy to one or more users, to a group, or to your entire organization.

- Each policy node includes a Global policy that applies default settings to your entire organization.

- For each policy node, you can edit the Global policy, assign one of Teams' predefined policies (if any), or create and assign a custom policy.

Index

muting
    chat messages, 183–184
    meeting attendees, 232, 235
    and unmuting audio, 224

N

.nef file extension, 143
Noise suppression option, 222
notifications. *See also* channel notifications;
    meeting notifications
    channel messages, 100–101
    customizing, 283–288
    receiving alerts, 18
.nrw file extension, 143
numbered list
    applying to channel messages, 89–91
    chat messages, 172, 174

O

.obj file extension, 142
.odp/.ods/.odt file extensions, 143
Office documents, adding as tabs, 113
Open dialog, uploading files from, 137–138
Open eBook file extension, 143
OpenOffice file extensions, 143
.orf file extension, 143
org-wide policy, 297
org-wide teams, 25, 30–31
Outlook
    channel conversations, 80, 86
    sharing channel messages to, 100–101
    sharing chat messages, 185
Outlook calendar. *See also* calendars
    joining meetings, 218
    private meetings, 200–201

P

.pages file extension, 142
panel vertical strip
    Teams desktop app, 6–7
    Teams web app, 3–4
.pano file extension, 143
Participants pane, pinning attendees to, 234
.pdf file extension, 142

PDF files, adding as tabs, 114
.pef file extension, 143
permissions
    customizing, 47–50
    customizing for apps, 288–289
    customizing for channels, 68
    and roles, 26
    and tasks, 28–29
personal apps
    accessing, 108
    described, 104
    installing and uninstalling, 109
phone audio, 221–222
phone numbers, blocking and unblocking,
    278–281
photo file extensions, 143
photos. *See also* Custom image background effect
    selecting for profile pictures, 11
    taking using mobile app, 11
.php* file extensions, 143
.pict file extension, 142
Pin to top command, 148
pinning
    app icons, 110
    attendees to Participants pane, 234
    channel messages, 100–101
    chat messages, 183–184
    files and folders to Files tab, 149
    meeting attendees, 231
    and unpinning channels, 71, 73
.ply file extension, 142
.png file extension, 143
policies
    assigning, 301–306
    for components, 297
    customizing, 299–301
    deleting, 301
    duplicating, 300
    group assignment ranking, 302
    precedence, 302
    settings, 295
    working with, 298–299
pop-out chat
    creating, 167
    defined, 164
.pot/.potm/,potx/ file extensions, 143
Power Apps, 105